THREE
WANDERING
POMS

LINDA BOOTHERSTONE

JACQUELINE GRIFFIN

ANGELA GRIFFIN

THE AUTHORS

Linda Bootherstone has spent most of her life exploring the world by motorcycle. She is now based in Port Lincoln, South Australia where she follows her other interests of art and music but also takes trips on her motorcycle whenever possible.
She has written two books previously and made several recordings of her own songs.

Following the weddings **Jacky Griffin** continued to travel and work in Australia and New Zealand before returning to England. She subsequently travelled in Africa and then settled in the UK. After a career in social work she is now retired and lives in Hampshire.

Unable to travel to the UK overland by motorbike because of the East and West Pakistan secession conflict, **Angela Griffin** and her husband, Geoff Branston, flew back to the UK, first settling in Hampshire. After training and working as a nurse for some years Angie had three children and is now a proud grandmother. Angie and Geoff have lived in Dorset for the last thirty years.

CONTENTS

ACKNOWLEDGMENTS

Piecing together all the memories after 40 years has been a difficult but rewarding task. Angela Griffin (later Branston), Jacky Griffin, and I have tried very hard to agree on what happened! We have been greatly helped by the following people and offer our heartfelt thanks.

Geoff Branston, Sandra Davis, Peter Roe, Dennis Hodges, Bob and Shirley Rowe, Andy Scott, Charlie Scott, Jim Knight, Viv and Deanna Johnson, Terry Bick, Trevor Green, Chris Witcombe.

Viola Wiedmann for editing.

Mary Gudzenovs for publishing assistance.

Linda 2013

INTRODUCTION

In 2005 I was in England visiting friends to say farewell before I left on an overland journey by motorcycle from my home in Spain back to Australia. In Dorset I caught up with two very good friends, Angie Branston (nee Griffin) and her sister Jacky Griffin. The three of us had not met all together for many years and Angie and her husband, Geoff, dug out some old slides and the diaries that Angie had kept while we were 'three wandering Poms' around Australia in the late 60s-early 70s. We had a hilarious evening trying to put names to long forgotten faces and matching them with the comments in Angie's notes.

In 2012, in the early hours of one winter morning I remembered that evening and thought how interesting it all was and that we should share those memories. The inspiration for writing the book, therefore, came from these diaries of Angela, the eldest of the two Griffin sisters. Jacky typed them up, added her own memories, and forwarded them to me, now living in South Australia.

The story, therefore, is related using three voices, all different and showing the characters of three young women who made an extraordinary journey around Australia, on motorbikes, at a time when many of the roads were unsealed. We had no back-up vehicles or mobile phones, only our youthful optimism and sense of adventure.

Please note that some of the places mentioned in our travels cannot be found on modern maps as new roads have been built. Also some of the smaller settlements no longer exist.

Linda 2013

MAP OF PLACES COVERED 1969-1971

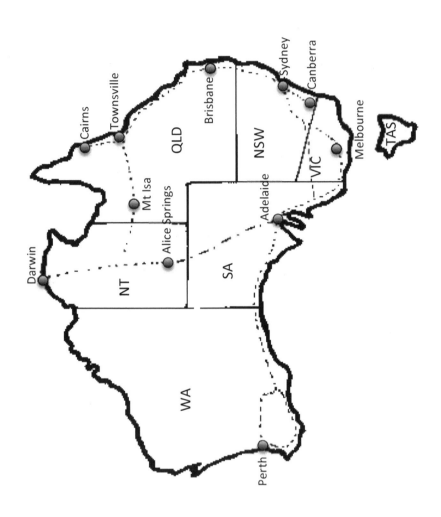

CHAPTER ONE

SOCIAL ENGINEERING

Linda:

It was a cold, wet night, normal conditions for January in London. The streets glistened in the steady rain, the streetlights making a monochrome picture of the dark pavements.

It was easy to park a motorcycle in the Strand; the rush hour had long gone and London was empty of traffic. Maneuvering the BMW into a space, I dismounted. I packed away my wet weather gear and used the mirror to dab on a bit of lipstick and tidy my hair before entering the grand foyer of the imposing building.

A woman with a wide smile and broad Antipodean twang welcomed me and ushered me into a room full of other young women. Tables were laid with tea and biscuits and colourful information brochures were scattered about.

My eyes roved around. I took in the scene, feeling somewhat scruffy in my jumper and trousers and motorcycle boots as most of the other women were neatly dressed in mini-skirts, stockings and shoes or the high boots fashionable at the time. They were made up with coiffured hair, not recently flattened by a helmet as was mine.

Smiling and nodding at a few of the groups that had gathered and were making polite conversation my eyes became drawn to two figures standing together, not talking but looking as lost as I felt. One girl was wearing a dark green vinyl coat. She had dark, curly hair, a pretty dimpled face and smiling mouth. The other girl was slightly shorter and dressed in a red, belted vinyl mackintosh. Her hair was long, straight and fair and as I approached I saw she had large hazel eyes with the longest lashes I'd ever seen. Both girls smiled at my approach, the latter girl slightly more hesitantly.

I held out my hand.

"Hello, I'm Linda from Sanderstead, South Croydon. How about you?"

They introduced themselves as sisters from Staines, Middlesex, but at present flatting in London. Their names were Angie (the dark one) and Jacky (the fair one) Griffin. No, they didn't know anyone else here and were quite happy to talk to me in this rather daunting situation in which we found ourselves. And why indeed were we here – herded, somewhat like sheep, into the enclosure of Australia House?

It was the late 1960s. The Australian Government had an immigration plan to entice workers to the country, more recently to enlarge the workforce for the booming automobile and white goods industry but indeed to attract skilled labour in many fields and to this end it was offering a passage to Australia for only ten pounds sterling, with the promise of help finding work and temporary accommodation on arrival while one did so. The only proviso was that one had to stay for two years otherwise the Government had to be reimbursed the full fare. All applicants needed to pass a strict medical, must be 'white' and have a clean police record.

What we didn't know at the time was that, as Australia had more men than women in that era, they were making a special effort to attract and bring over more single women as 'breeding stock'. So this is why we'd been accepted!

Over several cups of tea and a lot more biscuits than I should have indulged in, we shared our various reasons and plans for emigrating. Mine was simple. It didn't even involve looking for a rich station owner for a husband, nor even the thought of a better climate, although that did have a certain appeal nor the promise of easy to find employment or higher wages and standard of living. No, all I wanted was the chance to explore a new land on my motorbike.

At 23 I had already toured most of the British Isles and a lot of Western Europe, even so far as taking an unusual journey into Russia and it was on this trip to the FIM Rally in Moscow 1967 that I met two Australian guys who were touring the world on their BMW 600cc motorcycles. We met on the campsite in Moscow, shared our Russian adventures and kept in touch when they came to England where they stopped and worked for a while.

One, Harry Fillmore, continued on his trip over to Canada and the other, Trevor Green from Adelaide, decided to go back overland through Asia.

Trevor was a small, slight man almost dwarfed by his R60 BMW which had a huge 8 gallon tank for long distance riding. While working on a farm up in Derbyshire he met Jan Buckley who was a pump attendant in his local garage. On discovering she was from Newcastle, NSW he enquired,

"Would you like a lift home?"

"Why, yes, if you are going that way," she gamely replied, never having been on a bike before.

When Trevor brought Jan down to London to start the preparations for their overland journey they came to stay at my parents' home. Jan had a crowning glory of long, wavy, blonde hair but she had it all closely cropped the day before they left so it would fit under the spare helmet of mine that I had given her for the trip. Unfortunately she said later that, even with her short hair, the helmet was too small and she had a headache for 10,000 miles!

While they waded through the paperwork involved in getting visas and booking ships Trevor tried to talk me into going with them but I was having far too much fun at home and declined. He did, however leave some immigration forms from Australia House with me.

"It would only cost 10 pounds," he said, "if you come on the boat, and you can bring your bike too."

After Trevor and Jan left I thought about it for a few months and then decided to apply. I was still living at home with my parents and three siblings and, although earning a good wage as a Market Research interviewer and having a lot of fun with my fellow motorcycle club members (Saltbox MCC, Biggin Hill, Kent) I thought it would be an opportunity to further spread my wings.

My application was accepted and I awaited news of my passage. It was to be on the MV *Oriana*, flagship of the P&O fleet and I was to leave in March 1969. Trevor and Jan were already in Australia, Trevor in Adelaide and Jan in Newcastle. My ship would dock in Melbourne. This was as much as I knew when I rode up to my induction meeting at Australia House that evening and met Angie and Jacky for the first time.

As we had this great adventure in common and seemed to form a bond we agreed to keep in touch and they invited me to visit them at their address in London at a later date.

This I did and was very impressed at their independence from their family. I thought them very sophisticated; they even had contact lenses and prescription sunglasses! (not usual at that time)

Jacky:

I wasn't a big collector of fag cards. Quite why they are called that I don't know, probably originally came from fag (cigarette) packets but I did collect a series which were included with PG Tips tea. These were on Australia and I have a very vivid memory of standing in the back garden aged about 8 or 10 and looking at a picture of a koala bear or kangaroo (something suitably Australian) and thinking, "I am going to go there."

I was at a bit of a loss when I left college. Childhood had been 'difficult' and I didn't have much confidence. I worked locally as a secretary for a few months and then got a job as a coffee bar assistant in Butlins holiday camp at Bognor Regis. Conditions were pretty hard there but after a few months Angie joined me as she had left nursing. I recall that we seemed to spend a fair bit of time drinking with a couple of northern women, Newcastle Brown springs to mind as the tipple of choice. As the summer wore on we made plans to get a bedsit in London. We travelled up from Bognor and found a place near Gloucester Place. It was literally one room, shared toilet/bathroom. It had two single beds, two gas rings and a bedroom sink in the corner. I got a job at the Football Association in Lancaster Place as a secretary and Angie a job near Oxford Circus, also as a secretary.

We sometimes went to the Hundred Club in Oxford Street and, if we went home to Staines for a weekend, would go to a jazz club at Hampton Court. Angie was quite ill at one point and so went home to Staines and I was at the bedsit quite a lot on my own, but going home at weekends.

At the initial interview at Australia House you were supposed to give a urine sample and I couldn't. We had to get a cup of coffee before I could perform that feat! They asked us whereabouts we wanted to go and we said Sydney because it was the only place we knew the name of. I was aged 19 and Angie was 20.

I don't know if we had been given details of our passage before we were invited to Australia House to meet other 'single women' or not, but clearly we knew we were intending to go by ship because I remember having a conversation with Linda about luggage going in the hold and maybe not able to get to it. She joked about it not being any good if you had to go down to the hold to change your knickers. The nineteen year old me was shocked at how brazen she was. How small town was I!! Linda had approached us for a chat, we wouldn't have done that as we were not very outgoing at all! We were both good- looking, intelligent girls but lacking in self- confidence.

Linda came to visit us in our bedsit. She seemed a very strange woman – came on her motor bike – but I thought she was very sophisticated and worldly.

They sent us a telegram to tell us what ship we would be going on. It was around February 1969 and the ship was the *MV Aranda*, Shaw Saville Line. The journey was going to take six weeks and went through the Panama Canal. It felt momentous at the time!

CHAPTER TWO

LEAVING LIMEY

<u>Linda:</u>
My parents were unsurprised at my decision to go to Australia. They were well used to my wandering ways and were happy for me to take a look at the wider world. I remember our resident 'Tante,' a widowed friend of the family, saying,

"Here you are a big fish in a small sea. Let's see how you go when you are a small fish in a big sea."

I was 23 and it was about time I spread my wings and left the safe nest I had in the family house. My elder sister, Anne, had already married and moved away, my younger sister Janet, had been au-pairing in France. Philip, the baby brother, was just starting his first job and girlfriend and no-one was going to worry about me.

So, I just had to pack up or dispose of my few belongings, sell my car and arrange the shipment of my precious BMW motorbike, recently bought to replace the Triumphs I had owned. The bike was actually costing more for its shipment (£50) than my passage!

The hardest break was with my motorcycle friends at the Saltbox MCC. I had been on the committee for several years and was very involved in all their outings and social functions (hence Tante's comment). Most of them attended the large farewell party we had at my home to which Jacky and Angie and one of their sisters, Kathy, came and there were promises of plenty of letters exchanged – though few in fact were.

When the day came to depart, my parents drove me, with my sister Janet, to the docks at Southampton and I boarded the great ship with more smiles than tears as I was looking forward to the huge adventure. My voyage was to take 3½ weeks (unlike Jacky and Angie's six weeks via the Panama Canal) stopping at Lisbon and Cape Town, which sounded very exotic, and, after all, I was only expecting to be away two years to fulfill the Australian government's requirements. I had contacts to go to on my arrival in Melbourne and

Trevor Green and his family in Adelaide were expecting me some time later.

Jacky:

There was a great deal of excitement in the months leading up to the 'embarkation' and Angie and I would often go to Oxford Street late night shopping on a Thursday evening. About a week before we left Angie drove Mum's car to Knaresborough Place, to collect everything we had from the bedsit and wind it up. Angie was the born driver – took to it like the proverbial and had no problem driving into London.

We had to sort out everything we wanted to take which was probably most of our worldly possessions. We only had clothes really, not much else. I remember going to buy towels in Whiteley's. I got a red one and Angie a black one! We lived to regret those colour choices! We had nothing more in the way of household stuff.

It's very difficult to say what the family thought of us going. We were brought up in a very repressed household – nobody had emotions!! I would imagine that our sister Kathy would have missed us most of all because I think she was probably very lonely and in a pretty unrewarding marriage. The three of us seemed to get on pretty well at that time. Certainly, there was never any question, to my memory, of family trying to get us to change our minds.

It must have been about this time that the three of us made plans to share a flat in Sydney. Angela and I had intended travelling around Australia in a car but this idea must have got superseded by the possibility of doing it on a bike.

Linda had a going away party and Kathy came with us. The day before we left I know I had a big row with Angie and remember saying I didn't want to go to Australia with her. There was a sort of farewell dinner at our brother's the night before which our sister in law would have arranged. On the day, Dad took us to George V Dock (London) where the ship was. I think maybe Kathy came and Mum but don't remember who, if anybody, else. I cried my way onto the ship and as soon as Angie and I stepped onto it someone came forward and we were taken down to our cabin, a two berth, in the bowels of the ship and one of the first things we did was to put glasses up to the walls to try and hear what other people were saying!! (A little trick we had learnt at Butlins!) *A British holiday camp with cabins - Linda*

CHAPTER THREE

———

A LIFE ON THE OCEAN WAVES

Linda:
My ship was the *MV Oriana*, the flagship of the P&O fleet and was scheduled to take three and a half weeks on the voyage to Melbourne via Lisbon and Cape Town. It was spacious and, to me, luxurious, with a dining room, ball room and swimming pool. We were given three meals a day and there was always entertainment in the evening; dancing, quizzes and fancy dress. One night we had a cocktail party when we all met the Captain and wore our 'cocktail' dresses. During the day we could play deck quoits or go on a trip to the wheelhouse and of course, use the pool. I wasn't bored, in fact had a lot of fun meeting other passengers, mostly immigrants like myself, either single or young families and it was a huge learning experience to be thrown into a social life with people with whom I would not previously have come into contact, having mixed mainly with touring motorcyclists.

I met two brothers, Jim and Maurie Beresford, a couple of northern lads, who were travelling out to meet the rest of their family already in Australia. It transpired that Jacky, Angie and I were to become quite friendly with the whole family when we lived in Sydney.

For some reason Maurie gave me the nickname of 'Squirrel' maybe because I would run and hide in my cabin when I thought they were becoming a bit too 'fresh'.

I had my first bout of seasickness when we crossed the Bay of Biscay and was confined to my cabin for a while and it was during this time I learnt that two of my three other cabin mates were lesbians. Shock, horror. I hadn't met any before. One boasted that she had had a relationship with Dusty Springfield. However, I soon realized that they were quite ok and not likely to make any advances to me.

The ship docked in Lisbon and we were able to take a day on shore sightseeing around the busy port and also take a short excursion to a country village, brightly coloured with bougainvillea and sporting the local donkey and black- robed and be-scarfed inhabitants. I'm sure it stopped at the Canary Islands somewhere too but I really have no recollection of that, perhaps the women and donkeys were there instead of Lisbon.

The 'crossing the line' ceremony saw the crew dressing up as Neptune and his helpers who threw most of the young women into the pool. Lucky we had our bikinis on!

Unfortunately, prior to our stop in Cape Town I came down with a heavy cold, probably due to the air-conditioning, and had a perforated eardrum which prevented me from taking a trip on the cable car up Table Mountain.(The pressure on gaining height would have been dangerous). However, a look around the town was impressive with its Dutch- influenced architecture, the presence of mixed races and of course the view of the spectacular flat topped mountain towering over all.

Another bout of seasickness occurred as we rounded the Bight to our first port of call in Fremantle. I was welcomed at the dock by my friend Mick Sturgess who had come overland on his 500cc Velocette the previous year, sometimes meeting up with Trevor and Jan en route.

Mick was another Saltbox MCC member, who in fact, had accompanied me on the journey to Moscow in 1967. None of us knew exactly how old he was because he dressed in a different style from us. Instead of the usual T-shirt, jumper and jeans Mick always wore a white (well almost) shirt, jacket and trousers which hung loosely on his skinny frame. He had a quiet, contemplative air, would listen intently to others, while rolling a fag, then maybe burst into excited laughter.

He enjoyed going on the continental rallies and had decided to do the overland trip, actually only taking eight weeks to do so and travelling on the same ship as the London to Sydney car rallyists in that year of 1968.

He introduced me to my first Aussie friends on their home ground, Charlie and Carole Duffill.

"This is my friend, Linda," he said, "Miss-guided 1969".

I think he was referring to my decision to emigrate to Australia and stay the whole two years. He, having come under his own steam, could leave whenever he wished. A dyed in the wool Londoner, from

Battersea, he wanted to explore the country but had no intention of staying.

Charlie, also a keen motorcyclist, had spotted Mick's travel worn figure and bike sporting GB plates and befriended him taking him home to meet his wife.

Charlie was a big bear of a man with the typical Aussie beard and wide smile. He was a science lecturer at the local University and Carol was a librarian there. She was petite with dark hair and a slightly more reticent manner but equally welcoming.

I recall being somewhat puzzled when shown around their house. They had been married several years but still slept on a mattress on the floor. I didn't dare ask why they hadn't a bed.

My ship was only one day in Perth, a small isolated city at that time, and then I was back on the boat to Melbourne where my final disembarkation began. As an official immigrant with a UK passport the immigration procedure was no problem.

Fortunately I was met by the contacts I had been given and they safely stowed me and the few suitcases I had, in their car. I returned to the docks the next day to supervise the uncrating and fumigating of my BMW and soon had it roadworthy for the trip to Adelaide.

Jacky:

I had a very strong need to put on a "façade of confidence" as a youngster which had nothing to back it up. One example of this was on the first night on board the ship.

Our experience of eating out was confined to the Golden Egg or Wimpy where we would use the luncheon vouchers that I was given as part of my wages at the Football Association. It's easy to imagine how intimidated I felt in the ship's dining room on the first night when we were seated at a large circular table with about eight others. There was a white- coated waiter holding a big silver salver and when he approached me, he just stood there not making a move or saying anything.

I didn't know what to do so ended up saying, "Well, give me the spoon then!" To which of course he replied that he served me if I told him what I wanted. Good start then.

We weren't of course alone in not having experienced silver service dining before. As the journey progressed tales were told of people committing other social gaffes like trying to eat corn on the cob with knives and forks. We were smart enough not to order anything we didn't know.

The trip was great fun! I don't recall any organised entertainment. We made our own. This often consisted of sitting in the bar drinking with a crowd of fellows, all travelling on their own. They were all good people and we had a great time. As the weather warmed we sat by the pool in the sun. The first stop was Curacao which was pretty brief but an exotic place to us. The next was Barbados and we were played in by a steel band. A group of us walked in and around the town and ended up in a bar drinking delicious dark rum. There was a 'blue movie' (as it was called then) but Angie and I pretended not to watch it (conforming to the stereotypical "nice" girls) Not quite sure how much I would have been able to see anyway (that would have depended on whether I was wearing my contact lenses). I was pretty vain and didn't wear my glasses unless I had to. We drank that wonderful dark rum from the bottle on our way back to the ship. The following day we went to a place called 'Paradise Beach' which was the archetypal white sand, blue sea beach and I still have a lovely photograph of a crowd of us in a beachside bar.

We woke up one morning and on looking out were suddenly going through the Panama Canal. It was quite a sight and overwhelming, the steep sides of the canal towering alongside the ship. We stopped at Panama City which was again quite a shock. The police all looked to be seven feet tall and armed to boot! It all seemed very exciting and dangerous. Malcolm, one of the other passengers was getting off the ship here as he was a mountaineer and was travelling to do some more climbing in Lima, Peru. We thought him very daring.

Tahiti was where Angela had her 21st birthday. A group of us hired a car and drove round the Island which was quite beautiful, lush and idyllic. In the evening we went to Quinn's Bar which was right on the wharf very close to where the ship docked. The bar was something out of another world to us and certainly broadened our education. The ship's crew were set to enjoy themselves there and it was the first time I had seen men dressed as women – quite a sight for a 19 year old, who was old in some respects but unsophisticated in others!!

Linda:

I found a quote from Harold Stephens, Wolfend publishing: http://haroldstephens.wolfendenpublishing.com

Imagine an Old West saloon, a Dixieland cabaret in New Orleans, an Oriental taxi dance hall, a German beer garden and a Pigalle bistro in Paris. Combine them under one roof on a tropical island paradise in the South Seas. Take away the liquor-control board, the fire marshal, the building inspector, the health and sanitation inspector, the W.C.T.U. and the D.A.R. What remains is the wildest, wickedest, most carefree bar in the world – Quinn's Tahitian Hut." So starts an article in the February 1964 issue of *Argosy Magazine*. The author went on to describe some of the goings-on and a history of the bar along with some of the characters that frequented the place and an account of a list of happenings on a typical evening.

So Jacky and Angie's experiences of it were quite in keeping!

CHAPTER FOUR

AUSTRALIA'S SUNNY SHORE

<u>Linda:</u>
Not stopping long in Melbourne, I was soon on the road, with my bike, to Adelaide and having toured extensively in UK and Europe, the 500 mile journey from Melbourne to Adelaide did not worry me. Indeed it seemed easy being one straight road with not many towns in between and little traffic in comparison with the other side of the world! The scenery was certainly different though, miles and miles of open paddocks, mallee and gum trees that I was not familiar with and very intermittent service stations. I made the trip easily in one day and arrived at Trevor's house in Tea Tree Gully, a north eastern suburb of quiet leafy green Adelaide, dubbed, the 'City of Churches' (and parklands and pubs).

I was thrilled to see Trevor again and to meet his parents and quickly set about finding work so I could pay my board and lodging and save for my onward travel. I found a job as a car detailer in a small second hand car yard. The boss's wife was a bit of a tippler and would get me to buy her bottles of cream sherry, the contents of which she would drink out of a tea cup so her husband wouldn't know. She often gave me a nip or two as well and I would fall asleep in the heat of the interiors of the cars I was supposed to be cleaning.

The $15 a week wages seemed quite a lot to me at the time and I soon had adequate to register my bike with SA plates and prepare for my trip to Sydney to meet up with Jacky and Angie as arranged.

While staying with Trevor I came to meet some of the local motorcycle crowd: Peter Westerman, Artie Passals, Bob Jolly and his girlfriend, Helen Bidstrop and Geoff Branston.

One night some of the boys were going out kangaroo shooting and invited me along. I hate to say but they were all a bit drunk and all I can remember was racing round the blocks in their ute (pick-up) with them shining the spotlight and firing at anything that moved. I'm not sure how many they hit.

Another first for me was going to the drive-in movies. We went to see "To Sir with Love." A later drive-in movie was "Wake in Fright" in which the 'roo shoot resembled the one I had experienced.

Geoff was also a recent immigrant from Southampton, UK, and had a Hampshire accent. He was of medium build and had a distinctive cleft in his chin and light brown curly hair. A coach builder by trade he could always find work as a panel beater, anywhere in Australia. He owned a Bridgestone 350cc and was interested in moving to Sydney.

The Kangaroo Rally in Ballarat was en route. This was an iconic motorcycle meeting as, in those days motorcycle rallies in Australia were a rarity and this one would add to my international collection of rally badges and also be mentioned in the British motorcycle papers.

So, in the chilly winter days of June 1969, Geoff and I set off together to brave the frosty Ballarat campsite .

At the rally we also found Mick Sturgess who had finished his stint of working at Shark Bay in North West Australia and was now on the road with his Velocette again. We also met Dennis 'Ginge' Hodges who was on a DT1 Yamaha dirt bike but his first love was BSAs and he was busy talking British bikes with Mick. Ginge came from Maitland, NSW, he was obviously named for his red hair and he gave me his address for later contact.

After the rally Geoff and I continued the cold ride to Sydney where we found Jacky and Angie already set up in a flat in Potts Point just a few hundred yards from the teeming centre of the infamous Kings Cross.

The flat was tiny, in reality more of a bedsit for two and squeezing four in until Geoff (quickly) found his own accommodation, was quite a feat. Even when he left it was a squeeze; I had to sleep on my airbed on the floor between the two sofas that doubled as beds for Jacky and Angie. My biggest worry was having to leave the bike unguarded out on the street.

Jacky:
"We are waiting for Misses Angela and Jacqueline Griffin to come to the lounge for disembarkation procedures as they are holding the whole ship up!" – or words to that effect! – was what I remember waking up to the morning we docked in Sydney. Horror of horrors – we weren't the 'sort of people' who did anything to bring attention to

ourselves – and certainly not in any kind of way to inconvenience an entire ship! I remember the previous night walking round the deck and looking at the lights of Sydney and certainly feeling fairly anxious and full of trepidation at this panorama of lights. Surprising then that we both overslept – clearly one way of dealing with anxiety.

Mad scramble then up to the lounge and shame-facedly going through all the immigration procedures. The goodbyes had all been gone through the previous night. We sat on Circular Quay for what seemed like ages, waiting to be collected. The Quay seemed pretty empty, everybody else having dispersed. There was a newspaper/confectionery kiosk on the Quay and not to waste an opportunity I went up and asked if they had an A-Z of Sydney!! I was looked at with some incredulity – people not knowing what I was talking about. Don't think I came away with anything else either! (A-Zs are street maps of the major cities in UK)

At that time you were given one week's free accommodation and Angie and I were going to stay in a hostel for migrants in Marrickville. This was a fairly new modern looking building and we had a small room with two bunks, not unlike the ship's cabin. You were also given breakfast but this was taken in a local café (deli probably) and the menu was a source of wonderment to us. Mince on toast! How amazing! We used to settle for boiled eggs though.

This now kick-started the whole business of finding accommodation and jobs plus all the other stuff that goes along with moving to a new country. We found a little flat in Potts Point otherwise known as Kings Cross depending on whether you wanted to impress or not as Kings Cross was the 'red light' area of Sydney. It had a small lounge/bedsit with a little kitchen and bathroom. Tiny though it was it was still bigger than the bedsit in London.

CHAPTER FIVE

———

UP THE CROSS

Linda:
Our address was officially Potts Point, the up- market end of what was essentially the notorious Kings Cross. We were soon to find out about its celebrated night life and the plusses and minuses of living in the area. The plusses were, we were definitely near to the centre of the action. The brightly lit streets sported all kinds of restaurants, clubs and ice cream parlours. I had never seen so many flavours. The El Alamein circular, lighted fountain was quite spectacular too.

Many different nationalities roved the streets but the only black faces would have been those of African- American servicemen on R and R from the war in Vietnam in which the Aussie boys were also involved. Aboriginals did not frequent the city and the White Australia policy of the time kept other nations out.

The most exciting thing for us was the theatre which had the daring show 'Hair' on at the time. I was shocked at the stage nudity!

Apart from the ice-cream, we discovered all sorts of other culinary delights many of which were available in the 'delis', a term which was also new to us, the local convenience stores.

In England the only real takeaways at the time were the Wimpy Bars that served coffee and hamburgers, but their idea of a hamburger was a flat roll with small slabs of processed meat inside and a dollop of tomato sauce. Here a hamburger was a proper meal. For a start, properly cooked mince meat pattie was served in a crisp roll with lettuce and tomato but you could also have extras such as cheese or even egg added. They were a feast! And we also discovered the famous Aussie meat pies which were delicious and so warm and filling on a cold day.

A convenience food which came in handy for sandwiches was something called 'devon' in New South Wales and 'fritz' in South and West Australia. It was pressed luncheon meat that came in a roll and was quite long-lasting and cheap.

We all found work. Jacky and Angie were secretaries and I, having trained and had experience as a Market Research interviewer, was employed as such by a small MR firm which had its offices in Kirribilli, just under the Harbour Bridge on the northern shore, near the entrance to Luna Park.

The Market Research company was called Inview Pty Ltd and was owned and run by a Mrs Jean Straughan who was only a few years older than I but already had a very confident managerial manner. She had a degree in psychology, was recently married and ran a very tight shop. She wore the large framed glasses that were the fashion of the time and very brief miniskirts which showed off her slim, shapely legs and were, some rivals said, the reason she won so many jobs for the firm.

With my previous experience in MR in UK I had no trouble fitting in with the work there and it gave me the opportunity to quickly learn the suburbs of Sydney as I needed to move around the different areas as I interviewed, moving house to house with my questionnaires and folder.

Initially, I only had my motorbike as transport and, as we weren't allowed to wear trousers while interviewing. This caused a bit of a problem as I had to find a local toilet or even telephone box to change into my skirt. Sometimes I felt like Superman!

One day in 1969 I was knocking on a lot of doors and no-one was answering. I knew people were at home as I could hear the TV's going. Then it dawned on me that it was the day that Neil Armstrong walked on the moon! No wonder they didn't want to come to the door. I wish now I had knocked and knocked and asked someone to let me in to see the historic spectacle. As it was, alone on the street uncompleted questionnaires in hand, I missed it.

Initially I rode my bike across the Sydney Harbour Bridge to work each day, fumbling for the toll fee, but the firm later gave me a car, after we had moved from The Cross.

The minuses of our accommodation there, were mainly the size of the flat which was not suitable for three people and it was relatively expensive because of its central location. Plus I was also constantly worried about the bike being outside. We decided to move to a more peaceful and affordable area and did what most Poms (term for English people derived from 'Prisoners of Mother England' in transportation days) and Kiwis (New Zealanders - after their native bird) did at the time and moved to Bondi.

Jacky:

Most secretarial work seemed to come through agencies and so I signed up with one of those and started what turned out to be for me a seemingly endless trudge looking for work. Angie found a job pretty quickly but I became very downhearted going from interview to interview and the number eleven still stands out in my mind. One employer queried whether I was up to the job because of my lisp. At last, however, persistence paid off and I got a job with Yellow Express, a freight carrier in Pyrmont, a dock area in Sydney. I walked to and from work, and passing the pubs which had only fairly recently changed opening hours so it was no longer the 'six o'clock swill'. (*A term used in the old days when pubs closed at 6pm and the men drank as much as they could before that time.*) The pubs in Sydney were far different from what I had known, although we weren't 'pubbers' or drinkers of anything much at that time. (*That soon changed!*)

We were fairly frugal with our money and certainly didn't lash out on any luxuries like bedding. I can only assume we didn't bring anything much like that with us! Angie bought a hair dryer at a very reduced price because the hood was missing – can't think why we didn't take one with us! Perhaps we thought the wiring may be different. We also used to use newspapers to add to the meagre bedding!

There was never any issue for us about not feeling safe in Kings Cross at night. We wouldn't have been what would now be called 'party girls,' though I do recall us coming home and stopping off at the fish and chip shop and enjoying what Australia had to offer. We also discovered Peter's Yogurt and all sorts of wonderful flavours new to our Pommy taste buds, especially the multi-flavoured Ice cream- even Christmas pudding flavour!

Both Angela and I had full English driving licences which in those days were in the form of a little red book – quite complicated affairs really – you could drive a tractor but not a steam roller type of thing. Anyway these had to be converted to Australian driving licences and we dutifully took them to the driving licence/registration authorities, which I seem to recall was in Roseberry. After the initial formalities were out of the way we asked if we could drive a motorcycle on our new Australian licences. We were asked if we had been allowed to on our English licences to which we replied that we had. Of course we didn't know one end of a bike from another!

The flat in Potts Point was in a small terrace house which had been subdivided up and one night I answered the house doorbell to several men who said they were police from Darling Point. I answered with my usual scepticism (my oh my, I was only 19!) that they must have thought I had just jumped off the Christmas tree! But they were genuine for, apparently, other tenants had reported a burglary.

We only had a short tenancy but it wasn't long before Linda arrived with Geoff whom she had met in Adelaide. It was a tight squeeze – there was only enough room between the two beds for one person to lie on the floor! Geoff found lodgings very quickly but would walk through the Cross to see us and we used to ask him how many times he had been propositioned on the way over. Looking back on it I imagine I found all this close proximity of strangers quite perturbing – my background didn't exactly equip me for all these new experiences. However, shortly after Linda came, we got a flat in Bondi which was a two bedroom place perched on the edge of a cliff!

Linda:

We were all used to living or working in London so the hustle and bustle of the city of Sydney, then approximately 2.6 million people, did not phase us. Public transport in the centre was relatively easy to use and, once we had our own transport, we found the side roads and highways not too difficult to negotiate.

The icon of Sydney at that time and the main North/South throughway was the Sydney Harbour Bridge, the magnificent steel arch construction which takes rail, vehicular, bicycle and pedestrian traffic between the Central Business District and the North Shore. The bridge was designed and built by a firm from Middleborough, UK and opened in 1932. The design was influenced by the Hells Gate Bridge in New York, is the tallest steel arch in the world and the fifth longest spanning. We didn't know all these facts and figures at the time, just thought that is was pretty spectacular and that it graced the shorelines of Sydney's magnificent harbour where ocean-going ships came and went from Circular Quay, ferries carried commuters between south and north shores and yachts gracefully sailed up and down the harbour beneath its span.

We became aware that the southern suburbs (i.e. Bondi) were mainly where the poorer people, like us, lived and the northern suburbs such as Mosman and St Ives were the more sought after, posher places but, like any city, there was a mixture of people on both sides and we had no trouble finding friends on both shores and our way about.

CHAPTER SIX

BONDI WAVES

<u>Linda:</u>

The flat we found in Bondi was in a large house on a raised area away from but in sight of the beach. It wasn't as well furnished as our previous one but had plenty of room. The flats around us housed high-spirited Kiwis but we all got on fine.

I had arrived in Sydney at our Kings Cross abode in winter. By the time we moved into our Bondi flat it was approaching summer and warming up and we were able to feel the difference between an English summer and an Australian one.

Firstly, being on the lower end of the rental market our flat had neither air-conditioning or heating. Our bedrooms were to the rear of the buildings, facing east and the windows were louvres with no curtains.

Being an 'up with the sun' person I was finding it difficult to sleep after about 4.30 am in high summer, when the sun rose and shone straight into my room, the temperature rising with it. Conversely the evenings were not as long as in the UK. There was no twilight and it could be dark by 7.30pm. The heat in Sydney was also quite humid. We at once dispensed with our nylon tights and wore very little makeup, as we sweated more. Out came our summer dresses but we found they were mainly long sleeved or made of the wrong material; synthetics are no good in the heat. It was far more comfortable to wear sleeveless cotton dresses or shorts.

I lashed out and bought myself a lovely yellow, sleeveless dress to suit the weather and was feeling very bright and happy with it. We had a twin-tub washing machine in the flat and took it in turns to do the weekly wash. This week was Angie's turn – in went all our clothes and out came a bright yellow rag! My new dress was obviously not meant to be machine washed.

"Oops," said Angie and we all laughed about it, but we were more careful how things were washed. It was about this time that we discovered that washing things together with Angie and Jackie's black and red towels also wasn't such a great idea; the black or red dye ran and made our other clothes look rather yukky, to say the least.

Though we lived near the beach at Bondi and didn't mind trying for a tan, none of us were particularly drawn to the ocean nor were we very strong swimmers but we did like to go down to the beach and ogle the muscled, tanned male Surf Life Savers who strutted around in their tiny bathers chatting up the girls while waiting for a rip to carry one off so they could show their expertise.

There was another reason why we weren't so keen on swimming in the sea; there were sharks around and also, on certain beaches, a horrid type of jelly fish called a Portuguese Man of War or, in local terms, a bluebottle. They gave a nasty sting which could be serious in some cases. Other nasties we heard about further north in the shallows were rock fish, cleverly disguised: if trodden on their venom was so severe it could cause death.

If the sea scene wasn't enough to worry you there were land creatures, like spiders for example. The Red Back Spider (made famous by the song, 'There's a Red Back on the toilet seat when I was there last night') is a relatively small spider, the male of which has a distinctive red dot on its black back. The female, however is the venomous one, though smaller with no dot. They like to hang out in places like wood piles and, obviously, toilet seats, given that out-door ones (dunnies) are usually made with a wooden plank. I even found a nest of them under my BMW seat when it hadn't been raised for a while. They give a sting which can cause swelling and pain and can be fatal for babies. Huntsman spiders are bigger and hairier, not dangerous but quite scary to look at. Funnel Webs are also venomous but supposed to be just around on the North Shore, not having ventured over the Bridge.

In Bondi, some flats were riddled with cockroaches, another creature that we were unfamiliar with but soon got to know. Of course we soon learnt to take the Aeroguard (fly spray)with us everywhere we went and realized what a blessing fly screens on the doors and windows were. Also we became familiar with the scent of the circular, green mozzie coils put out at evening BBQs. Snakes we were warned about but I don't recollect ever coming across any. Mostly they were a problem if you lived in the Bush.

These were the not so pleasant Australian creatures but we soon saw kangaroos and koalas in the zoo before going bush ourselves and getting to know the Aussie birds was a joy. The warbling magpie, the laughing kookaburra and the more raucous 'kaa kaa' of the crow we soon learnt to recognize. Then going up into the Blue Mountains we heard the gentle 'ding ding" of the bell bird, a totally new delicate sound.

When I was given a car, a Toyota Corolla, automatic, by the firm, we were able to take trips together and explore the outskirts of sprawling Sydney. The Harbour Bridge was the escape route to the northern suburbs and more exciting Hawkesbury River region; the southern and western suburbs such as Parramatta, not so appealing. However we did explore them too and were initiated into the world of the RSL club and its poker machines by Maurie and Bruce Beresford and family, my friends from the ship. They were well ensconced in the western suburbs and happy to show us around. Although we enjoyed the cheap club drinks we never became addicted to the pokies.

On my forays out into the suburbs of Sydney looking for different social classes for my Market Research surveys, I became familiar with the middle class quarter-acre blocks in the outer suburbs upon which were built what we would call 'bungalows'- single storey houses. Because there was more land available, it was normal to build a house on a block and not fence it off. Coming from the 'privet-bush and fence' society in UK it was strange to see the houses set back on a large expanse of lawn with few flowers or shrubs and no front gate. The post box was not set in the front door but on a post at the edge of the road. This was for the convenience of the postie on his little bike to drop in the mail as he passed and the newspapers were just thrown out onto the lawn. The sprinklers that were set to move around the area were also a novelty.

However, the inner city suburbs had older buildings, more similar to the British style of terraced houses. Paddington was a cheap area at the time and many university students rented flats or shared houses there. On one of my many surveys I was invited in by some students, Dianne and Darius, and became friendly with them. They had a motorbike and often joined us on our runs (when we all had our motorbikes). They were co-habiting, very avante-guard in my eyes. Many years later I met them, a respectable married couple with kids, living in Adelaide.

The Rocks was another 'undesirable' area then. In the days of sailing ships and convicts the local bars were full of rough seamen and prostitutes. While undergoing a clean up process it was still not the trendy area it is today.

We were fascinated by the strange and often tongue twisting names; Woolloomooloo, Parramatta, Wagga Wagga etc. Though many areas were named after English places; Richmond, St Ives etc., they certainly didn't resemble them.

Having regained contact with Jan Buckley, the girl who came overland with Trevor, we all went up in the car one weekend to visit her in Newcastle (aptly named after the coal town on the East Coast of England) where she was living with her parents. Newcastle was an industrial town, well known for its coal but it was quite pretty and not too difficult to find our way around.

Jacky:

I remember going to visit Jan as she was having a party. There seemed to be a lot of confusion for us three as we were asked to bring a 'plate' -not sure how long it took us to sort that out! *(this is something that often confuses other nationalities when they first come to Australia. To 'bring a plate' means to contribute to the party by bringing a plate full of food – it is not an indication that the hosts are short of crockery, as we thought. We found one of the favourite 'plates' was a sweet dish called pavlova; white meringue, berries and cream which, apparently, was created in honour of Pavlova, the dancer, when she visited Australia.)*

The party was also the occasion, as I remember it, when the stories that we had been told about the men standing at one end of the room with the keg and the women down the other end, came true. We had taken to beer drinking in quite a big way by this time and inevitably we weren't too happy about this!

Linda:

The next day was overcast but warm and we went to a local beach, Caves Beach, I believe, spending hours swimming and collecting shells, not realizing that, though it was cloudy, the ultraviolet rays were cooking us. The hundred mile drive back to Sydney was agony as we were all red as lobsters and so sore. We soon learnt that the Aussie sun was not to be trifled with and ever after smothered ourselves with sun-cream.

Another Aussie habit that caused us some concern became apparent one day in Bondi.

Tony Harter was an Englishman who had joined our band and was flatting with Geoff and Mick in Bondi. He had a ute but had become interested in Speedway and wanted to buy a speedway bike. A local Aussie guy had one for sale and brought it round for Tony to view. After going out to see the bike in the back of their ute the boys invited him and his mate in for a beer and were chatting to him when one mentioned his girlfriend was outside. We girls were there in the flat and said, horrified

"Why didn't you invite her in too?"

The Aussie guy said; "Oh no, she'll be right'

We were amazed that this girl had been sitting alone for at least an hour in the ute while the boys chatted but couldn't help thinking that it was her own fault. There was no way we would not have invited ourselves in too!

We showed our Englishness in another way which confounded some of the Aussie boys.

Although it is now a well known commercial phenomena, in those days Valentine's Day was not very well known in Australia and certainly not in the English way of sending unsigned cards to members of the opposite sex indicating interest in them , if only in fun and, of course, anonymously.

We three girls bought cards for all the guys we knew, both English and Aussie and sent them. Of course, the English guys twigged our game immediately but the Aussies were perplexed, they'd never had a Valentine's card before!

Although the car was handy, my motorcycle was my preferred means of transport for pleasure and social life and Jacky and Angie saw the possibilities of us touring together on bikes which would be cheaper to run and much more exciting. Having joined the local motorcycle club and met other enthusiasts the girls eventually bought their own steeds; Angie a 350 Honda and Jacky a 180 Yamaha. We were soon taking regular rides out on Sundays with other motorcyclists that we had met through the Willoughby Club on the North shore. These included John Edwards, Brian Anderson, Richard Evans and a woman rider, Sandra Davis who lived in Frenches Forest with her husband, Gary and young daughter Cathy.

Sandra was also small and slim, with long fair hair, though a bit taller than me and she was a true motorcycle fanatic, not owning a car and doing all her family shopping by loading the bike with huge bags. She worked in a financial institution and seemed to have her head screwed on in that aspect as she had organized the mortgage on their attractive wooden house which stood on stilts in the leafy suburb.

Her sister, Deirdre Hatton, also slim and petite but with darker hair, also rode a bike and it came to our notice that there was to be a Road Safety Ride organized in both Sydney and Newcastle. Several local motorcycle shops sponsored it and they were calling for entries for both solo riders and teams.

Sandra, Deirdre and I entered as a Team and I entered in the over 500cc solo class. The competition was over two days. The first part comprised an extensive observed road course both in town and country, including dirt roads, and the second day saw us at Randwick Race Course area where we faced various skill riding and obstacle courses such as in and out of cones, riding over a see-saw, braking distances etc. The outcome was that we won the women's team award and I won the women's over 500cc award.

The prize for the solo ride was presented by Ryan's motorcycles of Parramatta and this gave me an idea when Sandra pointed out to me that there was to be a 'Powder Puff Derby' (a race for women only) at the next race meeting at Oran Park. Sandra had a 350 RD Yamaha which was suitable for the race track but my lumbering old BMW was a tourer rather than a racer.

"Why don't we enter?" said Sandra, looking excited.

"Well, I don't know, I have never raced before," I replied doubtfully.

"Go on, you can do it," she insisted. "I'll enter if you will."

In order to be competitive I needed a faster, lighter bike. On the strength of my win with their award I fronted up at Ryan's, spoke to the manager and came away with the promise of a loan of a prepared 250 Suzuki Savage for the race. I was a sponsored rider!

The day of the race dawned and with much excitement we were all gathered at Oran Park.

Out of the 10 entrants the most experienced and keen favourite was Peggy Hyde from Victoria on her 500cc Kawasaki. She won with a clear lead from start to finish but Sandra and I held the spectator interest and the commentator's main spiel as we were dicing for 2nd place the whole time. With her extra 100cc she was ahead on the straight but I would catch her up, late braking into the bends, was almost alongside on the exit and then she would draw away again. She beat me - but it was a close thing. My audacity at bend entry was mainly due to the fact that the Teflon slide in the carburettor was jamming the throttle open and I was having the devil's- own trouble shutting it down in time for the bends!

This was the first and last time I raced at Oran Park but the experience was to stand me in good stead for my later racing career in Perth.

Meanwhile Jacky and Angie were getting more experience on the road, both dirt and bitumen. We took rides up through Galton Gorge to Wiseman's Ferry and also out on the rough roads to Jenolan and Wombeyan caves. Though new to motorcycling the girls both became proficient in a relatively short time.

We also took rides out to Wallacia museum, Warragamba Dam, La Perouse and Botany Bay, determined to see as much of this part of Australia as possible while we were living there.

In January 1970 we made use of the Australia Day long weekend to ride over to South Australia where the Southern Cross Rally was being held close to Adelaide. Some of the members of the Willoughby Club were going also, including Sandra, on her Yamaha. I rode my BMW but Angie and Jacky, having smaller bikes, thought the distance would be too much in the short time allowed and were happy to go pillion with the boys. When we arrived I was delighted to be able to introduce them to my Adelaide acquaintances, and friends I had made while I was living there before going to Sydney.

When we returned to Sydney, we all gave in our notices and started preparing for our ride to Western Australia. Much as we enjoyed living in Sydney, and had made many friends there, we wanted to move on and had decided to try living in Perth.

Jacky:

We hadn't been in Bondi long before we started looking into Angie and me buying bikes. Linda made connections with local bike groups. Certainly I remember John Edwards who Linda met through the Willoughby Club which was on Sydney's north shore. There was a chap called Stan who worked in a motorcycle shop in Parramatta and there is a photo of me practising in a local park on a 180 Yamaha which I subsequently bought.

Certainly my experience of riding a bike was pretty traumatic. Angela had taken to car driving much quicker than me and likewise with motorcycles. I have always been a slow learner with anything mechanical and I really found it very daunting and scary trying to get used to the bike. We went on various day trips on the bike, sometimes meeting other motorcyclists who were all good fellows and who we kept in touch with. The whole riding experience was pretty difficult for a long time. One weekend we went to Canberra and I managed to propel myself over the handlebars onto gravel. This didn't do much for my looks! That was the weekend we met Greg Miekle and his friend, Peter Roe, people who we would in the future stay with – their families all being very hospitable. (*Linda :We met the two boys at Coffer Dam outside Canberra. Greg was on a Triumph T100 and Peter on his new Honda 350. We, of course, gave them our contact address in Sydney. They came to visit us there and stayed for a while with Geoff, Tony and Mick in their flat and joined us in a New Year's Eve party with the Willoughby Club members.*)

Linda had instigated much of our social life through meeting motorcyclists and it became a bit of habit that a few of them would come round to our flat on a Thursday evening and have a few beers. She had also met a fellow on the ship, Jim Beresford who was living in Sydney with his parents so we got to know his family. It was the Beresfords who introduced us to their RSL Club (Returned Soldiers League), another Aussie phenomena, and were very welcoming to us.

Geoff was living in Bondi with two other English guys, Mick Sturgess and Tony Harter, so you can see how we built up a network of male friends. The only other female I recall us knowing was a young woman called Sandra who was also a motorcyclist. She was married and lived in the suburbs with her husband and young daughter. Linda got interested in motorcycle racing and we used to go to Oran Park for her to practise. We would take our lunch which was whatever faddy diet we were on at that stage – grapefruit followed by hard- boiled eggs come to mind!

Linda at the Kangaroo Rally, 1969

Jacky learning to ride with Geoff

Angie, Sandra, Linda and Jacky, Sydney

Greg, Pete and Linda, Canberra,

Sandra and Linda, racing at Oran Park

Angie, Linda and Jacky outside Bondi House

Sandra, Angie and Brian Anderson

Mick Sturgess and his Velocette

Training run around Sydney countryside

Linda with company car, Bondi

Brian Anderson and his BMW

Angie, Jacky and Sandra at Oran Park, 1970

Angie on her Honda, 1970

Sandra (rider 200) in the Road Safety Ride, Sydney, 1970

Richard Evans, Linda, Angie, Brian Anderson, Geoff Branston

Geoff, Mick, Angie, Jacky and Linda

Angie cleaning her bike

SYDNEY TO MELBOURNE 1970

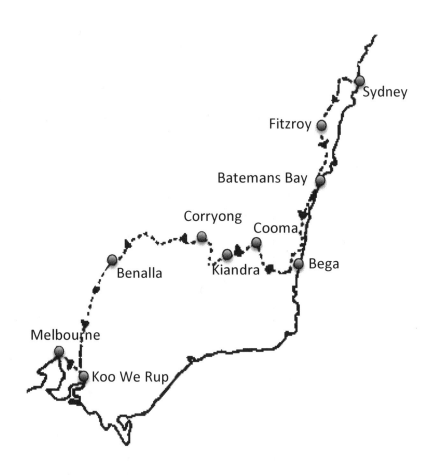

CHAPTER SEVEN

———

SYDNEY TO MELBOURNE

Linda:

Angie and Jacky felt confident that they could undertake the trip to Perth on their bikes, Angie perhaps more so than Jacky who was not quite so self-confident, but I was sure they would be fine and would enjoy it once they were on the road.

We had the bikes organised for carrying out tents, clothes, spares and supplies. Angie's 350 twin Honda and Jacky's little 180 Yamaha trail bike were both able to accommodate throw over-canvas saddlebags that could be lined with plastic bags. I had fixed, hide saddlebags on my BMW (previously on a NSW police bike).

I had an Optimus petrol stove that we could use for cooking and we had inflatable air mattresses and sleeping bags for our night-time comfort. All set with maps and our sense of adventure, we were set to go.

Angie's Diaries:

Wednesday 18/3/70

Wednesday morning departed tail intact. *(Jacky- this refers to fox's tail Angie had found and tied to carrier on her bike)* Utensils packed in un-waterproof ex-army saddle bags and tool bag. Petrol can on Jacky's carrier. Photo and goodbye session with Dave and Chris (our neighbours from the flats). Brought spare clutch and throttle cables and bulbs for Honda and Yamaha. Denis altered BMW suspension. Departed once again at 11.45 a.m.

Filled up outside Parramatta. 8768 miles on clock. Made good progress. Rained Fitzroy Falls donned wet gear and it stopped raining. Just practice you know. Arrived Batemans Bay as the sun was setting. Tired and cheerful. Stayed camping site for $1. Eaten by mosquitos. Demolished tin of soup, and Limits (weight watchers biscuits) and coffee. Wonder what variety of soup it'll be tomorrow. Filled up at 8906 miles took 1 ½ gals to do 138 miles.

Thursday 19/3/70

Fellow caravaner banged on tent (if it's possible) at 6.00am. Got up to coffee and one Limit biscuit. Dew heavy. Dried out tent on the swings. Snapped Jacky on swings reverting to her childhood. Packed, took some photos of the Bay. Left with 8943 miles on clock. Boy what a start to a glorious day! Rained and rained. Everyone and everything got soaked. Roads even and straight. Jacky was ahead had ridden Honda earlier. Whilst riding her Yam Richard's tape came streaming out of pocket of khaki jacket and was flying like the Union Jack on carnival day. Wrapped itself completely round the bike and me. Clancy Brothers fluttering in the breeze. Could hardly unwind it for killing myself laughing. Round sprocket, foot levers, front wheel. Wonder if Richard will still speak to us!

Couldn't get the BMW to go – rain driving down in buckets. BMW wouldn't start – changed to Jacky's spark plugs. The Yam losing all its speed. Pushed the BMW down hill physically then alongside with Honda. Started – Linda away. Turned the Honda and dropped it TWICE. Tut tut. Left some petrol on the road. Jacky returned to see what was up. We were saturated through to our knickers. She had us lined up with a cup of cha in the bakery at the next town. Dutch people and they gave us bread that had got a bit burnt on top and a big tub or marge which we ate standing in the boiling (lovely) bakehouse. Felt like heaven. Carried on. Got water in the Honda starter motor and it was igniting as the engine was going. Linda came back. Yam not going well. Averaging 35-40 mph. Stopped raining. Linda and I dried out the starter motor, me overseeing not fit for anything else. Dried and re-assembled twice, then success.

123 miles - 1 ½ gals at Bega.

Too wet, saturated for anything, so got a cabin (Cooma) $3.75 for the night. Covered the Honda with space blanket. Biscuits and coffee in communal kitchen and played cards with 4 PMG and other blokes. Went to bed 8.30pm. Money well spent. Clothes wet all night and still in the morning. Discovered I'd lost my fox's tail… sob sob…

Honda started pulling back earlier in the day. Terrible I thought, stopped altogether. I thought help, help. Linda came back and we stood there getting more and more worried as it sounded real bad. Then thoughts of towing or flagging down a truck. I said perhaps I should have put it on reserve petrol!!! How stupid can you get? We laughed so much with relief. Kick me, kick me I said. As Linda punched me on the nose!

(Jacky - I just remember this day as being very, very wet and I have a distinct memory of a baker working in his bakery having just brought us in from the wet — lovely, lovely man!)

Friday 20/3/70/21/22

Started off for the Snowy Mtns. No rain – soon changed! Tried changing plugs on Jacky's bike – no good. Only firing on one cylinder. Conjures up horrible thoughts of serious baddies. (Note true Aussie word). We left about 8.45 am, all in wet weather gear and woollens. Started climbing the mountains. 9154 took 2 gals. Was so wet all over forgot about the rain trickling down the neck arms and seeping up the leather boots knee high. What you can become immune to after being wet for so long. The bike was crawling and tiring and annoying Jacky so much it was ridiculous. So taking turns, Jacky took the Honda, Linda the Yam and me the BMW. Got to Kiandra where we'd originally hoped to reach the night before. A ski resort, lift as well. Coming into it, we were glad we hadn't reached it. Desolate and shanty-town looking! Rough old wooden and metal sheeting shacks – looked like a mining town.

Bike with white fairing went by looked like a cop so obviously didn't wave. So far only seen two now three bikes out this far. Obviously not common by the look we get from the local yokels. Stopped at the pub-cum-hotel-cum tourist kiosk. Brought a Snowy postcard. Pie and coffee. Then as part payment had to listen to the woman serving raving on about the worst part of the journey to come. The highest mountain – which turned out to be high above cloud level. Oh what fun – nearest we'll get to shaking hands with the angels (the good ones and the bad (hell) ones). First time they'd had rain for ages etc., etc. Knew we were coming of course!

Filled up. Jacky's bike – eventually, after the man in the bar condescended to come out. Off into the rain again and nothing in sight but gloomy impending mountains looked like a Welsh mining town. Just got away from Kiandra, Linda off after gathering speed from a downhill burn up. Jacky before me. Getting up speed in third gear and the BMW went into its infamous wobble. What a nasty feeling, the whole front shaking violently from side to side and no arm pressure will hold it still or even help a bit. Slammed down the gears. Just missing Jacky expecting to shoot off a narrow bridge at the bottom of the hill. Stopped and becalmed myself after beckoning on a lorry and Landrover, the occupants of whom thought I was mad. Oh well, it often does not do to worry. So off again.

(*Linda: The pre-1970 BMWs had Earls forks which had bearings in them. If these bearings or the headraces had any play the bike would sometimes unexpectedly go into a wobble. They earned the name of BMwobbleyous. It was a trait that was quite exciting at times, as Angie found out!*))

Caught up Jacky and we started some steep, windy descents. The rain still merrily sheeting down. Coming to a round smooth bend and the bike started its BMW wobble. Hells bells. Down to second and the steering was first non-existent. Straight off the road and onto the mud and logs and ditches which lay on the bend. I felt all the weight of the bike behind the reverberating handlebars which I was madly trying to cling onto. This is it I thought – trees and an almighty drop looked to be my epitaph. I could feel the weight of the luggage on the back lurching violently as the bike hit a mud bank and went sideways. It was no good braking or stopping. It would have crashed. So I held the throttle open, my heart had stopped seconds ago and my eyes were staring madly ahead frightened even to think lest something else loomed ahead. The bike just leapt and smacked everything in front and I think it was only the sheer weight of it that ploughed it through. How I got back on the road upright I'll never know. I noticed a car flash by and imagined them at Kiandra revelling in the gory details of seeing a motor cyclist bite the alpine mud and meet the dizzy perishing air of a few thousand feet drop. My stomach was knotted I felt bloody terrified. What the hell am I doing on the god forsaken mountain. Naturally from thence on (no I didn't become converted) I rode at 10-15 mph.

Jacky and Linda, whom I found after a few painful slow miles, were waiting and I then did a swop. The Yammy could only take upgrades at about 5 mph and in 1st gear but boy did I make up for it on the down hills and bends. The clouds were low or rather the mountains were high and we missed some fantastic scenery. The Snowy Mountain dam scheme was a wonderful engineering and building achievement, at that time it could have been the crown jewels and we wouldn't have noticed (second thoughts – perhaps we would). Suddenly after coming round a bend and descending the road was clear – no fog. No rain and it looked as if there was radiant sunshine glistening through the newly washed trees and bushes and plants which lined the straight smooth white radiant forest pathway. I leapt off my frothing steed and as Jacky and Linda came down made them pose by the sign "Snow is not cleared from this point onwards." This referred to the route which we had just covered and had taken us several hours. I felt so cheerful after having got through, although Linda's remarks at Kiandra "Don't worry Jacky, it couldn't get any worse" were fateful. Little did we know then!

The oil in the Yammy was practically non-existent and I, having noticed some oil drums in some workman's lorry we'd just passed, I went back and they very kindly gave me some engine oil. Refusing payment, he said; "It's the shire's not mine" and grinned. Oh what a happy man.

Another 20 or so miles and we were at Corryong where we all filled up. 9245 miles and 1 ½ pints of oil and some petrol in Honda and oil and petrol in the other two and we set off about 5.00pm at 35 mph to do another 100 odd miles to Benalla and friends. What an incentive. My face scarf would be just dried out from the wind when it would rain again.

We were all back on our own bikes now, having learnt I no longer had a front light. Jacky's legs wet as no over-trousers and her corduroy shoes worn to paper and damp with it! It was a nightmare of a ride for Jacky. We kept her pace so she was in front and I was behind driving by her headlight and Linda behind, trying to camouflage me from the cops as I didn't fancy being stopped not having any registration or disc. Jacky's headlamp is twisted to the left and so consequently she went off onto the dirt track which lines the roads out here. I, not being able to see followed! While Linda bowled up alongside and said, "What you playing at?"

Linda:

As we were making our way through the cold and cloudy highlands little did we realise that we were passing by the largest engineering project undertaken in Australia. Perhaps we could be forgiven as only 2% of these works were visible above ground.

The Snowy Mountain Scheme was devised in 1946, after WW2 and, in 1949 a New Zealand-born engineer William Hudson was chosen to lead the work. The idea was to capture, at high elevation, the water of the Snowy River and some of its tributaries and divert it into the Murray River and Murrumbidgee River via two tunnels cut through the Snowy Mountains and then passing through two hydro-electric power stations. In this manner not only would power be generated for ACT, NSW and VIC but extra water in the Murray and Murrumbidgee would help water supply, drought relief and irrigation for the agricultural production in the river valleys. Two important towns were constructed for the scheme; Cabramurra, the highest town in Australia, and Khancoban. Cooma became the headquarters for the project. Development in the area enabled the birth of ski resorts in Thredbo and Guthega.

The scheme covered 5124 sq. kms, almost entirely in Kosciusko National Park. A huge project, it was foreseen that a great number of workers would be needed and William Hudson was directed to recruit them from overseas. After WW2 Europe was in dire straits with many unemployed so men were found from over 30 different countries. This obviously had an effect on the cultural mix of Australia as 70% of the workers were immigrants.

The living conditions were very hard, men living in tents or flimsy temporary buildings that were moved from site to site as construction demanded. Many of the workers left families behind in Europe, sending money home or waiting until they had enough saved to bring them over. The women who did come battled isolation and freezing conditions and worked hard themselves to establish homes and a sense of community.

Over the 25 years of the scheme's construction more than 120 workers died but most of the living remained to settle in Australia. When finished in 1974 (four years after we rode through) there were 16 major dams, 7 power stations, a pumping station and 225 kms of tunnel, pipelines and aqueducts. The Snowy Mountain Scheme is seen as "a defining point in Australian history and an important symbol of Australian identity as an independent, multicultural and resourceful country" and we missed it as we rode through in the clouds!

Two songs I have heard are indicative of the cultural mix and the scarcity of women at this time. The first song, 'The Cooma Cavalier' by Ulrick O'Boyle sung by the Settlers on Macca's Top 100 album. The second song is:

'Rocking the Cradle' (I am a young man from the town of Kiandra) a traditional Irish song adapted by singer Sally Sloane of Taralba, that indicates the doubtful parentage of the baby in a marriage where the wife runs around.

I am a young man from the town of Kiandra
I took a young woman to comfort me home
But she goes out and leaves me and cruelly deceives me
And leaves me with a baby that's none of me own

Oh the day, rue the day ever I married
Oh how I wish I was single again
For it's weeping and wailing and rocking the cradle
And nursing a baby that's none of me own

While I'm at work me wife's out on the ran tan
On the ran tan with a handsome young man
Yes, she goes out and leaves me and cruelly deceives me
And leaves me with a baby that's none of me own

On with our ride......

Angie Diaries:

Friday 20/3/70 continued

Reached a sign "Benalla 25 miles" and simultaneously Jacky and I shouted and madly waved our arms. Eureka! Arrived at Greg's place about 9.00pm and Mrs Mieckle couldn't get over how wet we were, then all the packs. All day Saturday and Sunday she had chairs and clothes rack covered and draped with clothes, air beds and sleeping bags. The room (lounge) no less, hit 110 degrees at one stage and a steady 95 for the rest! We slept on the floor with Greg's and Ken's sleeping bags and damp air beds. Greg and Pete plus girlfriends surveying us as we tried to sleep that Friday night feeling fat and contented after a wonderful meal of soup, eggs and sausages and mounds of bread and coffee. Sheer luxury!

Next day Greg tried to solve the Yamaha's problem. Plus the aid of his friends, Bill and Don, and about five others. Greg's bike had caught fire at the Wine Festival they went to as they drained the petrol from his 'Triumphant' and as the last drop came down the fumes met the tilly lamp a few feet away and bang it was all over for no longer troubled 'Triumphant'. The charred remains are now lying in state in the garage and I <u>mean</u> charred.

New clutch cable on – very good. Pistons and rings taken out

Sunday – no better. Carbies cleaned – no better. Greg had his 'Triumphant' which he had brought from a friend John in Melbourne, yet to reassemble with new rings in time to get him back to work at Melbourne Sunday.

Saturday night Pete, Don and Bill took Jacky, Linda and me to the Albany – band and pub 25 miles away at Waggarandall. Finished 12.00 went for coffee in a road house on the way back. Nice to be in a car while the rain belted outside. My how we felt sorry for the motorcyclists outside! We haven't eaten so well or felt so much as if we were at home than this weekend. Three meals a day and while we've enjoyed it we'll be glad to get back to our diet of biscuits, soup and coffee incredulous as it might sound.

Pete solved the Yamaha problem after we'd conditioned ourselves to the fact that the Yamaha would have to be freighted over to Adelaide (blocked mufflers). Had a go on Denis' 450 Honda – lovely. Steering was right out after a prang (another true Aussie word) he'd had. Greg left this evening Sunday, after successfully reassembling his bike for Melbourne. Now watching Johnny Cash at San Quentin Jail on telly. Ken (Greg's brother) Pete, Mrs Mieckle and us. We're setting off tomorrow morning for Melbourne. 65 miles to gal.

Jacky: I have a memory of a day that really pushed me to my limits in terms of riding (which didn't come easy to me) dreadful conditions etc. I clearly remember lying 'in bed' on Mrs Meikles lounge room floor and Greg etc. coming in, raising my head and dropping it again! Also remember exclaiming at Mrs Miekle's electric frying pan! (these weren't used in UK, so were new to us).

23/3/70
9406 miles Benalla
9509 = 1 ½ gals .76c
9620 = 1 3/4gals .80c Koo-Wee-Rup

Bill came round in the morning to say goodbye. Loaded up and left about 9.00. My bike missing badly at about 60mph but nothing serious so carried on. Supplied with chewing gum. Don't like it much but might come in handy (puncture?!) Must get new watch strap as buckle fell off in sleeping bag. Good day, bit nippy, lovely scenery. Hills flanking the sides of the road ended up doing 214 miles to Lang Lang in search of "The Shell Shack". Old map and went out of our way. Turned back at a town where monument erected to Hume and

Hovell "who paved this way" they weren't the only ones but at the wrong time (couple of hundred years to be precise) and going in the wrong direction.

I've got so many cuts and blisters on my hands they look like shredded radishes. Went round some lovely bends and wooded scenery. Down some hills. Thick forest looked like scenes from Hans Andersons Fairy Tales. Beautiful while the sun was still out. Parrots shot across the road in front of us. Started raining in the afternoon – donned wet trousers. Very difficult trying to get directions from Australians, "just up the road" – (at least 20 miles) Left and right – meaning right and left. Adds a bit of spice I suppose.

Filled up at Koo Wee Rup. Found the Bass Highway and Shell Shack and were we pleased to see it. Now the burning question – were they in? Mr and Mrs Pen were serving. It's a typical petrol station with café and living accommodation. Set back off the road a good U-turn drive-in surrounded by fields. (an un-Aussie word) Got the subject round to having nowhere to stay and so after meeting George Sheriff originally from Tasmania, a character and a half, we ventured 500 yards down the road when his old Austin broke down. So he and Linda conferred under the bonnet for a few hours. Meanwhile, Beryl and Ken rolled up (the friends of Mum and Dad's from England). Saw some of their slides that evening and a good chin wag about Ferry Avenue and escapades. Promised to go and see George in his shack the next morning after the trip to see the setting sun went amiss.

24/3/70

Linda still can't discover the cause of my bike missing. Went to George's. He paints quite well. About 67 a real character – lives on top of a hill overlooking French Island which is next to Philip Island (the race meeting circuit). Beautiful view for miles. He looks after about 100 cattle - Fresians and Herefords. Drives about the paddocks in his old Austin about 50 mph over the bumps. One of the cows woke him up this morning, half way in the caravan. Building a corrugated shed, no floor, looks like a Gents and Ladies. Got a boat about 90 years old ex-naval lifeboat going to sail it. Used to do motorbike stunt racing.

We went up on our bikes. Found a cow's horn which I am going to sandpaper and varnish. Went back and said farewells and followed Beryl and Ken to Silverdale where we brought our tent $43.90 then went to Beryl's sister Susan, got a small baby. Very different to Beryl. Left there and went into Melbourne. Gave us an address of some friends of theirs in Perth.

What a laugh in the city. The looks – unbelievable – mind you we do look like three didecoys. Looked round the shops and got looked at. Jacky brought some wet weather trousers. Linda, a spoon (collects them.) Me – my watch strap, 25 cent postcards and kept going back to Coles for the free biscuit samples! Left 5.30 pm and went to Barbara's Aunt's (girl Linda met on the ship). She said she's married – well what do you know – everybody's doing it. So after coffee and biscuits found Barbara's place and are now kipping on the floor. Jacky and Linda impatiently waiting for me to turn out the light.

Driving along with the trams is a bit hairy. Yellow and red flashing lights everywhere so go through them regardless.

9830 full tank at Lorne.

(Jacky: Remember quite clearly the stark contrast between driving for miles in the bush/country and the not very nice city).

25/3/70

Sitting on the back of BMW writing this. Funny in Melbourne the lights go from red to amber then green as in England. But in NSW go from red straight to green – very dangerous. The points on my bike are very badly pitted as yesterday. Linda manicured them. Bike won't start. 3c to use the loo in Melbourne. Useless bit of information for would-be tourers. People seem friendly enough.

Whoops another tram bites the dust! We'd get looks even from a dog dressed the way we are. Brought new points $7.88. Ugh. New film. Chatted up the Honda salesman (English from Brom). Said give $4.00 for my Honda – cheeky. Best bet, obviously, to sell privately. Jacky cashed the cheque from the landlords bond $40.00 just waiting for it to bounce. Harley Davison in an Ariel frame, one Pete talking about, in Honda shop window for advert purposes.

Thinking we'll have to buy some food as it looks like we'll be staying at Barbara and Gary's place again tonight – God knows what they're going to say or the look on their faces when they turn into the flats and see our bikes and baggage strewn all across the lovely clean, tidy flat block front. Had some eats and then off to the Captain Cook's Cottage brought out from England.

Went back to Thornbury and wheeled bike into gutter, had all the tools across the pavement. Couldn't get the Philips screws out so I'm nominated to entice one of the men from over the road on the building site over. "Oooh, what big muscles you've got – could you please help us?" or something like that. Anyway after dragging him back a second time we all fancied him. Oil everywhere and our hopes of succeeding diminishing fast. Spirits low we went to phone up a motor cycle shop – the owners whom Linda had met at the Kangaroo Rally. A slim chance, although we were broken down 40 miles away. Very helpful at giving directions to nearest shops – no hope there. Old bag opened telephone kiosk door, doesn't she know there's more important things than the fire brigade for her cat! Returned to discover Jacky had been chatting up our tiling friend who offered the use of his van (what about the bike!) to get the bike to a nearby shop.

Waiting outside, oil everywhere, and Barbara and Gary turned in "what happened?" eyes agog! Had the Honda half hanging out of the combie van and he kept driving too near the parked cars and pedestrians. What a scream! Linda followed and after unloading it – they said couldn't do it. So with pathetic eyes I pushed the bike up and they started to look at it – nearly 5.30. After a bit of a laugh and wires altered the coil was hot on one side, left and the left point wasn't sparking. Frightened the coil might be burned out! Lot of mint. Anyway discovered one of the wires from the coil to the points was shorting as it was rubbing in contact with the petrol tank. Pete had taken the tank off before at Benalla to fit a new throttle cable and they had probably come adrift. Still Linda very successfully fitted new points so it was only the cable that was making it miss. Gave him some money for a drink as he wouldn't take anything.

Shot back to the flat hoping no cops in sight as illegal not to wear crash hat – plaits flying and turned off Elizabeth Street up a one way street and a man from the cycle shop came rushing out waving his arms, you can't park here! So Jacky and Linda did a U turn while I went in and sought out the points for the bike. Got to keep the cops happy. Had a lovely chicken dinner and wine we'd bought.

Melbourne to Adelaide
Angie and Jacky – 1970

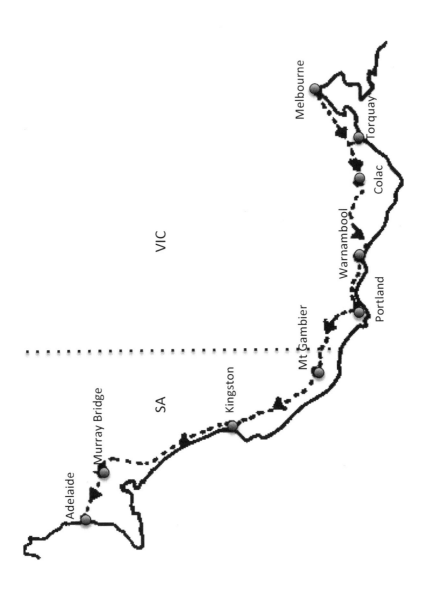

Melbourne

Torquay

Colac

Warrnambool

VIC

Portland

Mt Gambier

Kingston

SA

Murray Bridge

Adelaide

Melbourne – Bathurst – Adelaide
Linda 1970

CHAPTER EIGHT

———

MELBOURNE TO ADELAIDE

Linda:
Although the girls had followed my and Sandra's racing career in Sydney, neither of them were interested in racing as much as I and said they would prefer to go straight on from Melbourne to Adelaide. It was therefore arranged that I would ride with them to Melbourne and then double back to Bathurst, watch the races over the holiday weekend and then cross the Hay Plains to catch up with them in Adelaide. We would then accompany Mick to Perth where he would catch his ship back to England. So we bade each other a fond farewell, they off on their unaccompanied journey westward and me to the east.

Angie's Diaries:
26/3/70
Off to Adelaide Jacky and I. Linda going up to Bathurst for the Easter weekend racing
9755(up to cycle shop and back 3 miles)
9732 start full tank 964 miles ridden to date
9972 1½ gals Warnambool 298 miles ridden today
Left Barbara's 8.30. Stalled Honda outside and had to kick start as battery flat. Felt right idiot as surrounded by kids and observed by workmen who helped me yesterday. How embarrassing. Praying it didn't miss. Left Linda about 9.20 after she had shown us out of Melbourne on the Princes Highway. Did about 60 mph into Geelong. Brought a 10c Shell map, and couldn't decide whether to take the Great Ocean Road or stick to the Highway. Decided in the end to follow the O Road half way. Beautiful scenery reminded me of Scotland. Lovely winding bends. So green, sheer drops. Road follows the coastline really breathtaking, thought how Linda would love this road. A real thrash. Tempted by the rolling bays of sun drenched sand and large blue waves of staying for the rest of the day. Towns

like Torquay, Anglesea, Lorne and Apollo Bay nice names. Thought of Brian on passing Andersons Creek cruising by surveying the countryside. Decided as time was going and the road being as bendy as paved plus some dirt we'd go at Apollo Bay north to the Highway at Colac. Stopped a bit later and had biscuits, saw a dead lizard. From then on Honda started missing at 60 mph. Ugh! I thought, plus a few four letter words.

We went through the State Forest of Vic, absolutely beautiful, looked how I would imagine Canada to be. But bloody awful if it was dark. Passed through Port Fairy and wanted to get to Portland so the last 57 miles from P. Fairy seemed like 150. My bike I could feel getting steadily worse. Got to camp site about 5.45 pm 75c. Put up the new tent, it doesn't have a ridge pole and is very baggy obviously we haven't got the knack. Went into the town, what a hole but like all small towns they're dead by 6.00 pm. Going to buy a hot meal in café and then able to sit in light for a bit before back to tent but at 90c expensive light, so had take-away fish and chips and coffee 35c. Cursing Jacky's bike when discovered my fault as I had the choke on. Fell into bed I mean onto air bed. Jacky's is leaking even through Linda's attempt at puncture mending. Man at garage informed us as Easter Friday no garages open all day. Hell's bells. What else can happen?

27/3/70

10036 full tank – filled up Mt Gambier - filled up Kingston

Am now writing this by Edward's Dunlop torch light. In our new French tent which is still sagging. My mudguard rear – due to the corner being too heavy when loaded as the supports can't take the weight which is screwed onto the rear registration plate which isn't surprising why it won't hold it. Tightened up some nuts and discovered the tool box container has been wrenched away as it's connected to the mudguard. Took some things out of the tool bag. Took the tank off and moved the wires a bit. As we had thought one might be shorting again. Then removed the point's cover and going to move one of the point's wires to its original cover as thought it might be pressing against cover. Discovered Linda had the very small spanner and I had the spanner which we had thought it was. Not having any pliers or anything else that might do left that, started it and it went so after having an outrageous time at the self-service pump and eventually getting the bloke out, as he wondered what all the fuss was. Set off with the can filled with about a gallon.

Literally hundreds of dead birds, wombats, lizards, snakes and possums at the sides of the road. Although signs for kangaroos and koalas crossing the road they didn't give us the pleasure of their company. Bike missing needless to say and speed decreased. Stopped altogether and so got tools out and fiddled about. Nobody stopped of course. Van stopped which was going other way. Three young boys came over grins on faces. Explained to them. One raced a Kawasaki no 26 going to find an open pub. Racing at Mt Gambier which was 8 miles away. Took tank off. No insulating tape so took off tape on front suspension and wrapped all round maze of wires under tank. Petrol started leaking. Tube between tank and outlet underneath split. Not surprising the times it's been off and rewound. So they had a piece and were able to swop easily (without getting finger caught – must be a knack somewhere Linda) then wired the clips on by using my hair grips. Changed the wire on the points by using my tweezers and four letter words (dead fiddly job. Anyway it then roared into life after I put it on reserve. (I realised later that although at the time we all thought they'd mended it, it was only cos I hadn't put it on reserve, typical trick of mine as it's difficult to tell when It's missing and when it's short of petrol!) So perhaps the problem goes deeper as it's still just as bad. They decided to carry on into Mt Gambier as thought pubs might open for lunch. They told us the garages were open in Mt Gambier. Carried on. Jack stopped and rushed back to State Border signs for photos. Boys returned thought we were in trouble – nice of them, and took the Adelaide 296 miles sign which I had found broken off post and put across my Honda for photo.

Just outside town the screw came off Yam's muffler. Sounded as if she was in race came tearing past me to say funny noise – funny alright. Knocked it back on with the one screw driver we had and a rock. Sounds a bit more legal. Went into BP garage and filled up told that no garage open applied to Victoria and of course we were then in SA – sighed with relief! Had some food – naughty, naughty. Carried on very slowly only getting 40-50 mph now. Two motor cyclists waved and as we were stopped came back although not very friendly. Didn't know anything about Hondas so went on. Man on scooter waved. Quite hot now although comfortable.

Bet Linda's at Bathurst now wonder who she is with, we miss her.

Aiming for Kingston. Long flat yellow boring road and at only 45 bloody annoying for Jacky and me. Hope I'm not doing irreparable damage to bike. Looked at Jacky in mirror and she is riding along with left elbow resting on straight handlebar and cupping her chin, nearly died laughing – she looked as if she was out for a Sunday stroll.!!

In Millicent – what a laugh – first garage, "Do you know anything about bikes? " "No", But up the road next garage supposedly a Honda dealer. "Sorry mechanic not here try next garage" – mechanic on duty, car mechanic no good on bike. Anyway, got him to tighten Yam's mufflers. Noise dropped. Carried on and bike packed up. "This is it I thought – wait here till Tuesday," had the camp site arranged next to the BP garage. Jacky came back and said we'd have to go back to garage. Can't get it out of 1st gear. I then realised I'd forgotten to put the petrol on! Looked at the lever and it was split and nearly off. Needed welding. Swinging people there, pathetic looks – is it possible to do it now? Luck in – very nice bloke – real dishy too. Welded it for nothing - yes very dishy. Ice cream later and off. Anyway made Kingston. Set up tent opposite sea in park 90c. Had meal in café which she reckoned up cheaper than what it was. Jacky thinking crash hat had got tighter digged me in the ribs nearly back from café - haven't got gloves – look inside your hat I said.

(Jacky: Kingston had a beautiful camp site which was quite idyllic and right on the beach.)

28/3/70

10214 full tank 7.30am 10308 1 ¾ miles

Took 2 ½ hours to do 94 miles from Kingston to Meningie. Woke up 6.45 I realised had lost ½ hour cross to SA. Therefore we were able to leave campsite 7.30 and proceeded to crawl at 35-40 mph about 89 miles to Meningie. Had started to spit so pulled on all jumpers and wet weather gear to an audience of campers and caravaners. It was terrible we were crawling along. Pouring with rain both getting so frustrated and annoyed. I looked down to the right of the bike to find the spark plug lead to the black cap just hanging – no wonder going so slow with only sparking on one side. So stopped – a relief to both of us and took some more insulating tape off the front suspension and taped it roughly together. Couldn't believe it when I got back on – had this been the cause of the trouble all along? Nothing to do with the points or shorting wires under tank. I was now flying along at 60 and no missing. This was sheer heaven. I felt like hugging the bike.

Bowled into Meningie at about 10.00 and what a horrible trip it is from Kingston to Meningie. Once you get around Policeman's Point it is all swamp and bog and the sea grey and miserable curdling at the side of the road and a smell of rotting vegetation. Roads so deserted. We both thought how awful it would be to break down at night there. Had a pie and coffee in a BP garage and filled up. Got the bloke to tighten the mufflers on Jacky's bike as keep coming loose. Wonder how Linda is getting on – in the pub of course by now. Carried on my bike I think because of the rain and vibration was not connecting properly so missing again. Crossed the Murray Bridge and realised I'd been across it before on John's BMW – peculiar bridge I think. 51 miles to Adelaide and they seemed like ages. Black clouds everywhere. Being so near I was getting really excited and couldn't wait to see everybody.

Jacky brought a map of Adelaide. Got caught in a bit of traffic. Not surprising- Easter Saturday. Reached the bottom of the hill and Portrush Road. Phoned Trev who said "Cor you must be wet", but we weren't miserable any more – the sheer relief of reaching Adelaide I felt that brightened I could have started again. (Feeling that didn't stay for long though) Les gone to Bathurst, Geoff, we discovered gone with Pete to Mt Gambier. Tony with Trev, both working on bikes. So after getting Andy's address which was just down the Portrush Road off we went to see him and Mick. Lovely to see them I couldn't stop grinning – coffee and warmth – soft chairs and beautiful carpets even if it looks like the sea) and sherry. Soon warmed up. Had a blissful bath and put on a dress and felt like a woman again. Had tea and Trev and Tony came round, surprise, surprise, so off we all went to the Glynde. Mick took my bike and Jacky went on Andy's bike. Very good there, singers and large room and tables and chairs. Danced and then came back about 11.30 and sat up till 3.45 am talking, nay arguing. Dave and Chris saw Geoff. Worked out by my clock on bike covered since leaving Sydney 1645 miles. Now only 1700 to Perth – piece of cake!!!

29/3/70

Got up about 10.00am. Andy tuned up Jacky's Yam. Going like a rocket. Mick tightened mudguard and reconnected spark plug lead so won't have to buy another. Andy's wife Rose (*actually she was his girlfriend*) came round with David her baby son and her mother! The mother thought it was strange us two girls wandering around – not surprising I suppose. Sandpapered my cow's horn much smoother now. Am now covered in white horn dust.

About 3.30 pm heard from Chris, who came round, that Geoff was back from Mt Gambier so off we went to Pete Westerman's house. I felt terrible having Mick on the back makes me nervous. Great to see Geoff again. Pete was there (suppose he would be after all he does live there.) Talked, had tea, Mick went back to house and then to airport to see off his friend Frank who missed his aeroplane by 2 mins had hitchhiked down but managed to get a flight to Melbourne and then another from there. Seems most of his baggage consists of SA beer.

Saw some of Geoff's slides. Mick came back and as he hasn't any lights on the Velo we all left about 6.30 pm. Pete and Arthur racing at Mallalla circuit tomorrow. Cooked Vespa rice dish, Chinese plus a tin of Hungarian goulash. They said it was nice. Arthur came round for a bit was finishing off his bike that night for the morning. Chris round also. Washed my hair and does it feel good.

Bathurst cycle racing over Saturday and thinking that Linda will take two days to get back we're expecting her Monday/Tuesday. Going to Mallalla tomorrow. Geoff's going to weld the carrier and do the dent in the front mudguard one night next week.

Jacky – I have a vivid memory of following Mick back from the launderette . I kept seeing all these rags lying in the road and it wasn't till I caught him up that I realised it was his washing that was falling off the back of his bike carrier!

Linda:

Jacky and Angie stayed 6 days in Adelaide preparing their bikes for the trip to Perth with Mick. Mick was catching a ship back to England. They were waiting for me to arrive before setting off as I was due soon. As it transpired they had to leave without me.

ADELAIDE TO PERTH - 1970

CHAPTER NINE

———

ROADS TO PERTH

<u>Linda:</u>
I had heard that the Bathurst Races were the Australian Equivalent to the British Isle of Man T.T. races; a great gathering of motorcycle racing enthusiasts and the excuse for a few good parties at the mountain campsite where the spectators gathered.

Having left Jacky and Angie to their own trip to Adelaide I made my way to the picturesque town of Bathurst and was soon set up among the other campers to watch the races.

The racing was exciting but what sticks in my memory was waking in the morning to the sight of the valley below shrouded by mist with just the spire of the church showing through. A peaceful scene after the noise of the bikes the previous day.

Sharing beers with the other motorcyclists and swapping tall tales I met some West Australians and when I told them of my recent racing experiences at Oran Park and said I was heading to Perth they gave me their addresses there and told me the name of the secretary of the Racing Club of WA. I was to be sure and contact him when I arrived as there was an enthusiastic bunch of racers at the Wanneroo Park circuit. This contact was indeed to lead to an unexpected chapter in my life.

After the racing weekend was over I made my way West on the Mid Western Highway to Adelaide to join the others. However, crossing the flat, boring Hay Plains there was a dreadful bang and the bike cut out on one cylinder. As it was still running on the other I continued. I know now I should have stopped *immediately* but, as the road was devoid of any other human contact, not a car or house in sight and I was still in motion, I decided to carry on to the next services which were about 10 miles away. The BMW kept going and I arrived. When I switched off the engine and removed the plug from the dead cylinder there were metal filings everywhere, even coming out of the end of the exhaust pipe.

I knew the damage was serious and the bike could not be ridden but I had to get it and myself to Adelaide.

The truck stop at Balranald yielded my knight in shining armour. After asking around I found a truckie who was taking a load of metal rods through to Adelaide and would take me and the bike but this entailed getting the bike up on top of his load which meant using the loading ramp. Unfortunately this was the other side of the bridge and we had to tow the bike, rope tied to the handlebars with me on it. The bridge had wooden slats and I was terrified the front wheel would jam, I'd fall over, and the bike and I would be dragged along on our side, the driver unable to see us in his mirror. Fortunately, heart thumping, I kept the bike upright, we loaded it atop the metal rods and I took my seat next to the driver.

As we set off into the sunset the driver told me that he had gone over his allowed driving time because of a previous delay and was popping pills to keep himself awake. Would I please keep talking to help. Not a problem for me to chatter away but I was also nervous of being alone with this stranger and unable to escape if need be. I was wearing my two piece leather riding suit and kept it well zipped up!

But there were no incidents. Very late that night he pulled into Adelaide and took me home where his wife had a hot meal for us and made me up a comfy bed. In the morning I contacted the gang and they came round with a ute to pick me and the BMW up and start the strip down to assess the damage.

My continued riding after the bang, which was a dropped exhaust valve, had caused more damage as the metal had gone all through the engine. This meant not just a top end repair but a complete engine rebuild. Fortunately my friends in Adelaide, were able to help and spares were readily available.

Tony Harter was back in Adelaide and seemed to have taken a shine to me and was keen to show his engineering prowess so he helped a lot with the re-build. However, the delay caused me to miss the ride to Perth with Angela and Jacky and Mick, as Mick had his boat to UK to catch from Fremantle and couldn't wait. I would have to face the dreaded Nullarbor alone when the bike was rebuilt.

As it happened I was lucky because one of the Sydney boys, John Edwards, was visiting Adelaide and he had some time to spare on his holidays. When my bike was ready he kindly offered to escort me across the Nullarbor to make sure I was safe. What a gentleman!

Angie's diaries:
4/4/70 Adelaide
  10741 2 ½ gals Port Augusta 10881 2 ¼ gals   10673
  Left about 11.00am. Geoff had stayed the night so he was there at Andy's. Chris came round then Les, then Pete and Arthur and Tony. Left about 11.30am. A real depressing farewell. Jacky had a puncture about 30 miles outside Port Augusta and tried to flag down cars for an air pump about 1/3 stopped! Could be dying. Went to the pub till 10.30. Bike was missing badly I think a lot to do with the petrol. Alright in the afternoon. There's definitely something wrong somewhere. Eating too much as usual – no Limits
  5/4/70
  10980 1 ¼ gals 58c 1 pint
  11123 1 ¼ 80c 3.45 Ceduna 39c 11183
  In Penong 50 miles on the dirt 50 miles from Ceduna no price control therefore petrol can go up to 57c gal. Soft drinks 3c dearer. Left Port Augusta about 7.40am. All went right averaged 55-60 mph. Doing about 76 miles to gal at that speed. A strong wind. Saw a fox in the road tempted to whip off the tail for my bike. Also a dead kangaroo. Lots of dead birds and little animals. Beautiful coloured parrots, brilliant greens and reds, so strange not to see them in captivity. A town called Iron Knob nestling at the side of the mounts where they quarried the iron. Mick said the mountains had got smaller since he last passed them.
  Loads of signs at the side of the roads saying e.g. "charcoal paints a black picture" very subtle. Attempts at controlling the bush fires. Had a meal at Ceduna as Andy had said. Then hit the start of the 300 mile stretch of dirt. Took a photo of Mick and Jacky entering it. Not too bad. Have to concentrate for the pot holes – loose dirt. Most of the cars wave. All in the same mutual self-inflicted torture. Togetherness. Jacky lost the petrol can but retrieved it. Mick's things slipped. Tent and camera fell off the back of mine. Three drunk blokes gave Mick a drink of beer while he was waiting and then did a fantastic U turn sweeping up all the dust. Thought they were going to turn it over.
  Reached Penong at night fall. Mick discovering a puncture now mended. Offered the use of the railway goods shed. Could hear the mice and birds. Zoo with it. 250 population. Real bush town. Keep thinking there's going to be snakes everywhere. Hope they're friendly!

Wrote some letters. It's a lot warmer now. About 1200 miles to Perth now. Sat outside bar with local yokels drinking their beer. Them being rude to the customers as they came for petrol – dead funny. They came back to goods-shed didn't get to sleep till about 2.00. What a laugh.

6/4/70

11233 left Penong 11285 1 ¼ gals 57c Standard 48c a gal

Left 8.00am Koonalda 3.45 pm

Standard 54c per gal 11454 1 ½ gals

On the dirt for 250 miles. Most of it not too bad averaging 40 mph. Some hairy moments with only an open throttle to get you out upright. People waving. Dust absolutely everywhere. Brought 2 pkts of Limits at Nundroo on the Nullarbor. My conscience is everywhere. Have re-learned I need a tape-recorder on the bike as I think of so many things I want to write down but forget such as Mick tightening all his things. How my camera fell off, then the tent – good job Jacky was behind. Chain guard broken in one place rattles like hell. Hate to think what the vibrations doing to the bike. Dust everywhere. Water catchment tanks appear 20 miles. No rain since about October.

I developed a slow puncture so with only about 60 miles to go carried on just pumping it up. Went through some sand really deep. Just before Ivy Tanks. Mick only just got through it and then I only just managed it but Jacky came off in it and once more the gear lever took the worst part and bag fell open and nearly everything spread along the road.

(Jacky: I remember clearly coming off on the dirt and it seemed like a bit of an initiation but also a bit of a badge of pride as I only came off once on the whole 300 miles of dirt.)

7/4/70

11518 ¼ gal 47c standard 54c gal

11636 1 ½ 88c 11738 1 ½ 75c

Got out to Eucla before dark very relieved, very dusty. Purse full of it and still is. Had a lovely meal and very expensive like it was all along there like the petrol. Bike missing badly, Mick took off spark cap and just joined wires. No better. He rode it and me on Velo. Worked out how to get the best out of it. At Eucla stayed off the caravan park as it was all gravel. No grass anywhere. In the bushes. Rode through at night under the fences and moved the stones. Kept bumping into the German blokes, Alex and Jeanne and French Marcel. Met up with 2 other cars all going to Perth. Tasmanians, Hungarians and Yugoslavians drinking in bar loads of it. 3 cars started off for beach. Couldn't find it so Jacky and I went to bed. Mick had some lamb they'd stolen and rum nearby.

(Jacky: the caravan site was awful – all this hard horrible gravel – and had so looked forward to getting to Eucla – a big disappointment to me.)

8/4/70

11855 1 ½ gal 11978 1 ½ gal

Speedo gains approx. 3 miles to 120 miles covered. Very pleased done 80 miles to the gallon.

12037 ¾ gal

Left Balledonia ....Motel restaurant and bar at 8.00 covered 120 miles to Norseman by 10.00. Had coffee, filled up. Filled up again at Will. Mick discovered top of carburettor come off and so spent 20 mins doing that. Drew out $5. Heading for Kalgoorlie. Single track roads with wide expanse of dirt either side. Good enough run to Kalgoorlie. Telegraph poles along centre of high street. Some nice old style pubs. Sent some postcards.

Coming in to Boulder can see hill covered with industrial chimneys smoke billowing and lots of dirt heaps, disused quarries. Christ I am getting fed up with these flies, there's about 20 of them buzzing on and around me. Carried on to Coolgardie, Ghost Gold-Mining town. Spent a lot on making it into a tourist attraction. All afternoon practically looking in the goldfields exhibition and the Corner with old relics, cars, engines, wagons.

We were going to leave bikes just off caravan park, but in the washrooms and women said cost $1 for night. Like hell! Railway no good as trains coming through. Derelict house from the gold- rush days we decided on to accommodate us. Had a meal. Prices beginning to get back to normal city ones. Then into pub. Bloke started chatting. Drunk as a Lord. All his problems coming out. Discovered that the boarding house we'd put claim to belonged to him. Decided to ask him. He suggested railway shed and led the way. We all turned into a yard with a shed. Turned off engines and before we knew what was happening a New Australian appeared, shouting and swearing at us and waving a gun! We got the message alright but in the confusion I couldn't find my key. After what felt like ages we got the hell out down the godforsaken track until we came to a house where we discreetly (how you can be that with the Velo woofing and the Honda throbbing and the Yammy screaming) parked the vehicles under the trees. Our friend then opened the front door and we stealthily crept in, boards creaking. He showed us into a bar room and through the French windows we brought our bedding into our room. Very carefully we all laid our rugs, Indian style.

Morning and sounds coming from all sides so gathering our chattels we crept out with bated breath. Silently loading and then, setting the trusty steeds into roaring, deafening action we escaped. Jacky lost her scarf the previous evening, memories spread all over Aussie.

9/4/12

12130 1 ½ gals 12250 1 ½ gals

Southern Cross at 10.00am 12361 1 ¾ gals

Had coffee and toast (my how one appreciates the small things in life). Mick had a puncture which he mended. I withdrew $10. At Kellerberri had sandwiches. Jacky and Mick withdrew some money. From then on Jacky could only get about 45-50 mph. Once again we think that her mufflers are clogged again with carbon. Finished the rest of the 345 miles left to Perth we finished that day. Travelling approx. 50-60 mph. Arrived at Mundaring about 6.30pm at Don Chesham's, Nick's friend, fellow Velo owner and racer. He and his wife are a very nice couple. So lovely there, they put us up for the night. They've 7 boys and she loves every minute of it.

10/4/70

Bowled into Perth. Very windy. Tried for flats – no joy. Mick discovered *Achille Lauro* (his ship to UK) not leaving till Monday 13th. Absolute elation. Had a celebration cup of coffee and burger. Picked up mail. Marvelous – 2 letters from Mum, one from Linda, one from Andy, one from Dave, one from Kath (that's over Friday and Saturday). About 4.30 pm went to the place where Mick used to live. Were they surprised to see him!

(Jacky - We stayed at a house that Mick used to share with three fellas who I think had driven overland from UK. Trevor who was quite tall and had a Landrover, Chris, shorter with a beard and Trevor's brother whose name has left me)

Linda:

From Adelaide the ride up to Port Augusta was straight and boring but at least it gave me and John a last look at the top of Spencer Gulf. Port Augusta was the last main town before heading west. Ceduna on the west side of the top of the Eyre Peninsula would be the last time we saw bitumen in SA. From then on the dirt struck; 300 miles of potholes, bulldust and corrugations. I don't know how many times I fell off, probably a few, but it was certainly an experience and I was glad John was there to pick me up.

After a long day's ride and a night's camp in the Eucla sandhills John wished me bon route and turned back to face the dirt alone on his return journey.

I carried on West, passing through the mining towns of Kalgoorlie and Coolgardie which would have been pretty wild in those days of heady gambling on stocks and shares. I didn't do much sightseeing being alone, for my mind was set on reaching Perth and meeting up with the girls again.

Letter from Linda to Chris Witcombe in Adelaide explains the rest of the journey and an introduction to Perth:

29.4.70

Dear Chris,

Thanks for your letter. Nice to hear from you. Well, the last week and a half have been quite exhausting and we've only just settled in. I'll start from when I left Coolgardie as I wrote to Andy and Tony from there and you should have read that letter.

I stayed the night in a hotel in Coolgardie as it was pouring with rain and I was absolutely shattered. During the course of the evening I had my usual amount of sherry and had a good few games of dart winning half a chicken in the process. I also met a Scottish lad called Bill who was on a Bonneville and heading for Geelong. I told him horrific tales of the Nullarbor and gave him Andy's address.

The next morning was bright but very cold but at least it wasn't raining, for a change. The BMW was making terrible noises on the left hand side so I didn't take it above 60mph all the way to Perth. I arrived about 3pm and went to the only address I had which was of a fellow I met at Bathurst. I ended up down the pub with him and the fellows he lived with. He offered to lend me his bike (a

Bultaco) to race at Wanneroo Park, which I immediately accepted. Anyway, I spent the night at their house, going to a BBQ with them and then on Sunday started a search for Angie and Jacky. Eventually tracked them down at this address which is a real smart flat, at least it was till we moved in.

On Monday we all went out job hunting and Jacky got one almost immediately, typing in a psychiatric clinic. Angie and I weren't so lucky. I did get one which I started on Tuesday but gave away pretty quickly. It was with a Market Research company but not the same sort of work that I am used to. I was also getting increasing worried about my bike so I took the head off and discovered that the exhaust valve had seized in the guide so had to take it to the BMW shop to get the guide reamed again.

On Thursday Angie got a job at a Dry Cleaners driving a van and on Friday I was offered one as a receptionist in a car service place.

The weekend was very hectic. On Friday two boys came to stay with us, Dave and Terry. Dave lived in the flat above us in Bondi and had left a message for us at the G.P.O saying he had gone into the bush for a few weeks working on a drilling line. On Thursday he turned up with Terry as they had a few days off before returning to work in the Simpson Desert. They had nowhere to go so they stayed on our living room floor.

On Friday night we went into town and went to a night club after the pubs shut. I got sloshed and we didn't get back till about 2am. I went to bed but the others stayed up till about 4am talking.

On Saturday we messed around during the day getting my bike back together and changing Angie's tyre which was on wonky. That night the whole crowd of us went to find a party which didn't materialize so we came back here and were up till 3am again.

Sunday I went up to Wanneroo Park (*a circuit situated north of Perth outside the suburbs*) for a look at the track with Terry Bick, the Secretary of the MCRC. (*Motor Cycle Racing Club*) He is a real nice fellow and came out with us over the weekend drinking.

Sunday night I was absolutely shattered so went to bed at 9.30 and Dave and Terry (*our visitors*) were sitting out here writing letters. As I was lying in my bed I could hear this Irish Folk music coming from downstairs. It sounded like the Clancy Bros records. Eventually I couldn't stand it any longer and simply had to get dressed again and go down. I knocked on the door and asked if I could go in for a while. There were six fellows there, three of them Irish, one Scot and two English. One of them had a guitar, one a harmonica and spoons. Well, the long and the short of it was that Terry came downstairs too and we were up till 3.30 singing and drinking and it was absolutely terrific. I wished Mick (*Sturgess*) had been there, he would have loved every minute of it.

Well, not getting to bed till 4 I woke at 6.45 and had to face the fact that I was supposed to start work at 8. I decided it was too much effort so went and phoned them and said I didn't want the job. Then I had to go and find another one. I am now driving for a laundry and Dry Cleaners too. Yesterday we finished at 2.30 and today at 12.00!! Bloody good laugh it is too. The only trouble is that the money is terrible compared with what I was earning in Sydney. All the wages here are poor though our flat is only $3 cheaper than the Sydney one so we won't be saving anything. The thing is that I've only been here 10 days and have had more fun in those 10 days than I did in 10 months in Sydney. Everyone here is so friendly it's unbelievable. I think I'm really going to enjoy life here. The one thing that mars my bliss is the fact that my bike is still making horrible noises and is not going at all well. After spending all that money on it I am not at all happy. I think I will take the other cylinder head off this weekend and see if the valves are OK on that side. It really rattles like mad and has a horrible high pitched whine at times as though something is really tight. The thing is it starts first kick every time so I don't think the timing is out but the right exhaust pipe is very blue and it doesn't run properly on that side if you try it without the other cylinder running.

Problems, problems.

I hear you are working with Andy, how are things progressing there?

Tonight we are going out with the Shenton Park crowd, the fellows that Mick used to live with. One of them is catching the ship home tomorrow, the Oriana, which is the one I came on. We are going out pub crawling and with a bit of luck I may be able to see him off tomorrow if I finish work early again.

Dave and Terry left this morning at 4am to fly up to the camp. They have left half their clothes here for us to look after (and wear!) and we may see them in about three months.

Rod's bike won't be ready for Sunday so I am borrowing Terry Bick's 250 Ducati which I have never ridden and which has all the gears on the other side and the other way up so I'll be in right trouble with it. Also I can't practice till just before the race so God knows what a terrible fool I'm going to make of myself.

Could you please tell Tony and Andy they are right bastards for not having written. I posted their letter nearly 2 weeks ago so they should have got it by now. Are they getting on alright or have they poisoned each other yet?

Have any of you been out shooting recently? Our bunny tails are hanging on the wall and the feet are walking around all over the place.

Thanks again for writing, you'll all have to come up here, its great.

Love Linda

Perth seemed a nice clean city, more like a large country town, similar in size to Adelaide. Not too big and fairly close to the sea. The gardens at King's Park gave a clear view of the town as it nestled in the banks of the Swan River, which lived up to its name with black swans floating everywhere.

The flat that Jacky and Angie had found a first floor flat was in one of the northern suburbs. It was light and airy and, though small, it was more modern than the accommodation we'd had in Bondi and it had a safe area in which to park our bikes.

Mick and Jacky at Cocklebiddy

Linda at the WA border

Maurie Farmer on his Honda 750/4

Terry Bick with Linda's
BMWR60/5

MCTC run, Perth 1970

Angie and Geoff

Angie, Geoff, Jacky, Terry and Maurie

Linda striking a pose

Angie and Jacky

Linda on Terry's 250 Ducati

Linda relaxing on the beach, Perth
1970

Trevor and Jenny Luck

Charlie Hancock

Brian Cartwright with his Yamaha

Peter Senior with his Yamaha

Round the houses racing

Eric Nicol and Terry Bick on the Vincent

Andy Scott

Linda on Terry's Ducati

Terry Bick on 250 Ducati

CHAPTER TEN

———

LIFE AMONG THE SANDGROPERS

Jacky:
Angie and I had difficulty getting a flat in Perth for some reason.
Anyway, eventually we found one; two bedroom, somewhat soul-less,
modern, first- floor flat. Our luggage, remember we only had what
could fit on the bikes, had been shipped across to us free by the
courier firm I had worked for in Pyrmont, Sydney. I got a job
working and I suppose I was a civil servant as I worked for the
government/local authority as an audio typist in a child guidance
clinic. I made good friends with a woman I worked with, Jean
Horobin, who had had her fair share of problems with her children.

Linda:
Shortly afterwards I became a driver for Pacific Films. This was a
film processing company which had a stable of Volkswagen Beetles
which went around to the pharmacies in the city and suburbs of
Perth collecting the rolls of films that customers had deposited and
printing them in their laboratory in Subiaco.

There was also a run down to Bunbury and Busselton, about 100
miles south. This was a pleasant but monotonous trip and was done
leaving early in the morning and returning by lunchtime after which
the driver delivered back the processed films to the city pharmacies
whose films had been picked up in the morning. The run south was
on long stretches of single lane highway and was quite dangerous in
hot weather when, without air-conditioning in the car it was hard to
keep awake. Also during winter gales the air-tightness of the cars
caused them to be unstable and one girl died when her Beetle was
blown off the road into a tree.

The job enabled me to learn my way around Perth quite quickly
and I was issued with a smart blue dress as uniform. The uniform for
work was a particularly Oz phenomenon as, in UK at the time, it was
unusual to have uniforms at work; we all wore our own normal

clothes. I thought it was a great idea to have a uniform as I did not have many changes of clothes and did not like thinking about day-to -day dress so wearing the same thing was fine by me.

While working at Pacific films I met a young, red- headed woman named Charlie Hancock who worked in the laboratory and also rode the firm's scooter making some of the city deliveries. At a later stage she came to share our flat and we were amazed at her domesticity stocking the cupboards with things like flour and sugar, custard powder and spices, things we had never used. She in turn was amazed how little we spent on food and the effort cooking it. We lived on things like mince and cabbage. We were lucky to befriend her as she developed and printed all our, then black and white, photos and made enlargements of the ones we particularly liked. She became one of 'our mob' and later bought her own motorbike.

Perth in the 1970s had a population of around 700,000, more or less the same as Adelaide. The city was easy to negotiate and the suburbs gently sprawling in the sunny Mediterranean climate. Beaches were not far, a popular one being Scarborough where the waves were gentle and inviting.

Although much like Adelaide in size and population, Perth had a few differences which we found annoying to begin with. Firstly, the petrol stations all closed around 6pm leaving just one open on roster until about 10pm. If this was the other side of town and you were on your last drop it could be quite worrying. Also the pubs and restaurants all closed at 10pm and the only place you could get food after that was the pie stall by the Swan River. It became quite a late night hang-out.

As far as getting out of town it was an easy ride out to the higher regions of Mundaring where there was a weir and an explanation of the origins of the dam. Apparently it was designed by Charles Yelverton O'Connor, the engineer in charge of a scheme to provide water to the goldfields at Coolgardie. His forward-thinking design was much criticized, so much so that he committed suicide before the building was completed. The dam proved to be a great success and the saving of the industry and population at the goldfields.

After my initiation on Terry Bick's Ducati I very soon became a member of the Motor Cycle Racing Club which held regular race meetings at Wanneroo Park. The club consisted of a number of members who used a wide variety of machines to race ranging from a works Honda to a normal 250 street Yamaha.

Terry was a good looking young man, about 5'10" with dark wavy hair and a pleasant open manner. At age 24 he was a partner in a printing firm, Compact Print, and was the boss of a young apprentice, Greg Hastings, who later became a well known folk singer. However, I remember Greg as a young man who did bicycle racing and was surprised when he told me he shaved his legs! This apparently was to alleviate wind drag.

Terry raced his Ducati himself in the solo class but was also the swinger (sidecar occupant) for the West Australian sidecar champion, Eric Nicolls, who piloted his 1000cc Vincent powered outfit.

Races held at Wanneroo were mainly 'handicap' which meant that entrants were timed during practice to ascertain their mean speed and enable officials to decide at which intervals they were set off at the start, 'go' being the first, i.e. the slowest rider, and the fastest set off last and hopefully catching the others. This procedure was because there were not enough of any one class to hold individual races of 500cc, 250cc or 125cc. They were all mixed in together apart from the sidecars who had their own race. Some of the local characters were Pete Senior and Brian Cartwright, Ron MacIntyre (senior and junior) and Brian Cull, Don Chesson and Peter Fougere on solos and Trevor Luck on his outfit. There were others, of course.

The races were more of a social occasion as all the riders knew one another. The unsealed Nullarbor was a barrier to interstate riders participation so there was not much competition. There was no prize money involved, just a small trophy as a winner's cup and, at the finish of an event, a keg was tapped and I think more than a few of us drove home rather merry. It was the days before breathalyzers.

Occasionally there would be a 'round the houses' event organized. A country town would have its streets closed off and the corners lined with hay bales. The racers would ride these circuits dodging dogs and inattentive pedestrians. The parties at the end of the day included the locals and were great fun. Gnowangerup and Mt Barker were ones that we attended though only as spectators, cheering on Terry in his solo and sidecar efforts. However, at Wanneroo Park, on the 250 Ducati I was sent off 'go' in one race and managed to maintain the lead (scared stiff every time my boot scraped the tarmac on the bends) and won. The first and only time, I might add.

Another group that we joined in which we could all participate was the Motorcycle Touring Club of WA led by Maurie Farmer on his 750 Honda 4, considered a big touring bike at the time. We would hold club runs to many of the local sights and, on one occasion we treated a group of British sailors, whose ship was in Fremantle, to a sightseeing tour, taking them pillion for the day and being invited back to their ship, *HMS Hermione* (which the sailors called Hermy-one) for the evening 'rum rations'.

After the night with the neighbours downstairs and their music session, the Belfast Irish guitarist, Paddy, and I started singing regularly together and we began performing at the local folk club at the Shaftesbury Hotel in the centre of Perth. We joined some other local performers to form the Tin Shanty Bush Band in which I learnt to play the lagerphone, my first musical instrument, as I was formerly only on vocals. Our band preceded the now more famous Mucky Duck and The Bushwackers. Angie and Jacky were not singers but were an enthusiastic audience and Paddy's two housemates, Joe and Mick came along too.

I had always loved singing and was in my element at the folk club. As in motorcycling, folkies share a common bond and that means contacts in every country.

Jacky, Angie and I had not been in Perth very long before we were joined by Geoff Branston and Andy Scott from Adelaide. After our time together in Sydney and Adelaide, Geoff realized that he was in love with Angie and came over by train as his Bridgestone was in pieces and he was in a hurry to see her again. Andy, having split up with his girlfriend, Rose, wanted to try greener pastures so he rode his 125 Yamaha over.

After over 20 years of living in Australia Andy still had a broad Scottish accent and was a Scotch (and beer) drinker too. A well built guy, he was pretty wild and full of fun and he and Geoff often had some heavy drinking nights. The two boys shared a flat. As they were both panel beaters and mechanics they had no trouble finding work and Geoff, whilst working at the Honda dealer helped Jacky find a bigger bike. She swapped her 180 Yamaha for a 305 Honda Dream. It became obvious, after a while that Angie returned Geoff's feelings and they soon were seldom apart although, as was the norm in those days, not living together.

I put a foot wrong criticizing Geoff one morning when he was late showing up for an event we had planned. He was supposed to be a marshal.

"He's so irresponsible," I complained

Angie rounded on me, her eyes flashing. "So, you think you're so perfect then, Miss Goody Two-shoes?"

I'd never been called that before and was quite taken with the expression.

Meanwhile Terry Bick and I had been seeing a lot of each other, especially as we both had an interest in racing. I liked the way he started calling me "Darl" an abbreviation of darling which somehow sounded less threateningly soppy and more in tune with the Australian 'mateship' idea. He began inviting me back to his home with his parents for Sunday lunch and I was amazed that his mother still cooked on a wood stove, making delicious roasts with baked pumpkin, which I had never had with my Mum's roasts in England. Although the house was in the suburbs of Perth it had an outside dunny (toilet) quite usual in Australian towns but very unusual in UK by then.

Other vegetables that I and the girls were not familiar with to begin with were egg-plants (aubergines) and red/green peppers (capsicums) which were used quite a lot in Australian cooking. When I used to trail my mother around the local, Surrey St market in Croydon UK she made the rounds of all the stalls looking for bargains and the only veggies available then were the traditional local grown spuds, carrots, cauliflower, cabbage and Brussels sprouts. I had never seen anything as exotic as a pepper or an eggplant. It didn't take us long to try them out but cabbage remained the order of the day.

One drinking habit we were quick to catch on to was to learn to drink Aussie beer as the guys bought their rounds in jugs and if we didn't share that we missed out. Vodka and orange juice wasn't the same as the English style and glasses of sherry were too small and no good for the WA climate. So this was the beginning of our beer drinking career!

As far as dating was concerned, while Angie and I seemed to be spoken for, Jacky had many admirers but did not form any definite attachments.

My old BMW was becoming increasingly cantankerous and, with my 25th birthday looming, I decided to treat myself to a new one for this auspicious quarter century milestone. Going to the local BMW motorcycle dealer I traded my old 1960 R60 for a new R60/5 with an electric starter! Though a bigger, heavier bike I could still handle it and it was a joy not to have to spend time and energy jumping up and down on the kick start.

The Racing club boys only rode bikes on the track thinking us touring bikers were mad riding on the road where unknown drivers also came past in the opposite direction. However some of them were keen to join us on our social events and either came pillion or followed us in their utes. One such occasion was for my 25th birthday party when I gave the new BMW an outing, taking Terry pillion. Jacky and Angie rode their own bikes and Geoff and Andy came on Andy's 125, swapping places as rider and pillion as they rode along! Paddy, Joe and Mick came along in the back of Pete Seniors ute with Brian Cartwright as passenger.

Our destination was Margaret River, about 220 miles (300kms) south of Perth on the coast. Today, this is a celebrated wine growing area with many wineries and trendy cafes and restaurants and new houses but then it comprised just a pub and general store with a dirt track which led down to the beach. On arrival we set up our tents in the sand and then went back to the pub to check out the action.

A local club (Lions or Rotary, I believe) were holding a dance in the back room of the pub and we invited ourselves to join them, waltzing and quickstepping in our motorcycle boots to the strains of their string quartet. In the interval, when the band took a break we asked if we could sing and play as Paddy had his guitar and were given the OK. We played some lively songs with choruses so people could join in and the music was appreciated so much that we sang again in the next break.

To my great embarrassment, at the end of the evening Mick passed the hat around on our behalf for a donation and I immediately made an announcement that the money was to go to their club and thanked them very much for allowing us to play. Face saved, we very merrily piled into the back of Pete's ute for our drive down to the beach and collapsed in our tents. The next morning we were rather hung over and subdued on the ride back to Perth.

Another outing, which nearly ended in disaster, was a ride out on the bikes to a local recreation site. A little way out of Perth it was a lovely wooded area with a natural water pool, ideal for swimming on a hot day. We had taken our bathers and were laughingly splashing around in the cool water when Geoff decided to take a dive. He came up with his head streaming with water and blood! We rushed to get him out of the pool and on the bike to the nearest first aid spot.

The nurse there said: "The last person who did this died."

Angie, who had been white- faced and tight- lipped during the whole event, swallowed hard and breathed a sigh of relief when it was decreed it looked worse than it was. The nurse just put on a bandage and said it served as a reminder not to dive deeply in shallow pools.

One thing that I learnt in WA was that Poms were not universally accepted or even liked by some Australians. I could understand where the term 'whinging Pom' came from as I heard that many immigrants, especially women with young families, had found life too different in the suburbs and missed their families back home and consequently were never happy. However, I learnt that there was a reason deeper than that. Apparently some older Aussies had never forgiven Churchill for the debacle of Gallipoli and the great loss of Anzac troops. Perhaps this was more remembered in WA, as the troop ships had left from there. Anyway, I remember Terry saying his Dad would never employ a Pom.

We didn't let it worry us. Aussies had nicknames for everyone, the Italians were 'wogs' and all other Europeans were known as New Australians.

Another thing that we had noticed in Australia, which surprised and delighted us, were all the public holidays. There seemed to be more than in UK. Some being Australia Day, Anzac Day, Queens's Birthday, Labour Day and the normal Easter, Xmas and Boxing Day. It was nice to have a bit more time off. Also we noticed the custom of lottery tickets. Some people in England did 'The Pools' but lotteries were often done in groups at the workplace. Can't say we ever won anything!

We had a very full and varied life in Perth but were saving for the next trip: to go back East and then up to Queensland, across to the Centre and north to Darwin. At that time the road in the north of WA was unsealed and we knew that over 2000 miles of dirt was too much for our capabilities. We were still thinking in terms of only being in Australia for our two year migrant stint and then going back to UK, so we were determined to see as much of this huge land as we could. We had saved enough money during our time working in

Perth to be able to spend about three months on the road and see the other parts of Australia.

Not long before our planned departure, Jacky became ill and actually spent her 21st birthday in the Royal Perth hospital. We were all very worried about her but fortunately she recovered and we were able to pack up and depart for the first stage of our journey back to Adelaide. We were going to go via the South West of WA, through the Karri forests, along to Albany and Esperance before re-crossing the Nullarbor, this time all together and with Geoff there to pick us up.

I kissed Terry goodbye and promised I would keep in touch.

Jacky:

It was about this time I started to experience dreadful panic attacks, which only someone who has had them knows how debilitating and punishing these can be. I went to a local doctor who described me as 'confused' and I eventually ended up in the psychiatric ward of the Royal Perth Hospital for two months. This was the start of bouts of anxiety and depression that were to plague me all my life. All in all a pretty dreadful experience and one that none of us were emotionally mature enough to cope with.

Life went on and socially there must have been quite a lot going on. Angela was pretty serious about Geoff and Linda was seeing a lot of Terry. We were friendly with some Irish boys who lived downstairs and there was a thriving folk club scene which we all participated in, Linda more so as she was doing a fair bit of singing. I can't remember why in particular but I changed my 180 Yamaha to a 305 Honda Dream which felt more sturdy and solid.

Perth to Adelaide - 1971

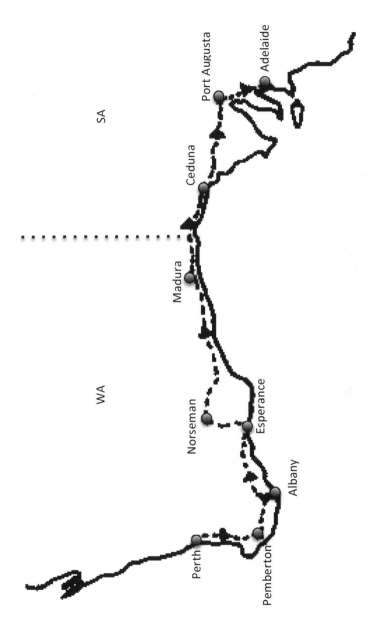

CHAPTER ELEVEN

BACK TO ADELAIDE

It was in the late summer months that we left Perth to return east but we were first heading south to explore the cooler regions around the SW of WA before facing the heat of the Nullarbor.

Angie:

Perth – Adelaide 1970

Left Perth fairly early after loading up. The last night, as we had vacated our flat, was spent in Paddy, Joe and Mick's place in the centre of Perth, where they had kindly given us refuge. The next day we had to sneak down the fire escape as the caretaker had got wind of our presence. All feeling a little the worse for wear from the leaving party. Three other Aussies joined us in the car park and we set off.

The route to the Nullarbor that had been decided on was the South West via Albany – Esperance turn right Norseman. It was great to be on the road again. The South Western Road through Pinjarra, Bunbury and on to Augusta. We took a break here and then headed toward Pemberton through the Karri forest stopping at a really tall one used as a fire lookout. Geoff climbed to the top using the metal spikes driven into the trunk with wire handrail spiralling to the platform above. Camping near Pemberton we had to do a little maintenance on Jacky's bike (charging fault). It had been a good ride 280 odd miles.

Started for Albany the next morning through Manjimup and Mt Barker arrived lunchtime, looked at the whaling station. Left Albany and headed east we camped near Ravensthorpe it had been a long day but enjoyable. Started early, (the Aussies left us here) and headed towards Esperance, Jacky Geoff and I had been alternating the pillion seat at various intervals from Perth. Passed Esperance and on to Norseman turned right for the Nullarbor and Adelaide a few petrol stops, arriving Madura late afternoon It was decided to stop here although Eucla had been our aim.

While packing up the next morning Geoff was adopted by a kitten who insisted on sitting on his shoulder and head. Ceduna was the next destination, refuelled Eucla start of the dirt. Our progress not so fast now corrugations and dust. Later that afternoon, Geoff and I were in front. A few trees started to appear on the horizon. As we approached a clump of trees 2-300 yards off the road on our left, three Aborignals came from under their shade, running and waving towards us. Curious we stopped. They were attempting to sell boomerangs for two dollars each. Geoff said he would have one if they proved they worked. Walking to the other side of the road he threw it. Sure enough it came back landing at his feet. It was purchased for A$2 in loose change - he wouldn't take a note. Jacky had arrived by then so we both shelled out our loose change for one each. We moved 5-600 yds further up the road into the shade of some trees, still in sight of the Aboriginals under their tree.

After a while Linda came into sight, still a long way off. The Nullarbor is very flat you can see for miles. As she neared, 'another sale' they thought, and left their shaded spot at speed waving the boomerangs. Instantly the BMW accelerated until she saw us in the shade of the trees and stopped.

Rest over, we set off again the trees were becoming more profuse the road surface was also changing to a very fine sandy top which in places could be quite deep 6-12 inches. Traffic, whilst sparse, threw up a huge dust cloud, which lingered in the air for ages. This loose bulldust surface also made it harder to steer the bikes. Jacky had come off twice-her bike had a good load on the back ,making it even harder to control. Therefore, in early evening it was decided not to continue into the dark and risk a broken limb. The bikes were parked a few feet apart on the side of the road and a flysheet put over the top, it smelt of oil and petrol all night, horrible! After a not very good night's sleep we headed for Ceduna and Adelaide. We made Ceduna in less than two hours back on the bitumen again.

On arriving in Adelaide, Jacky, Linda and I stayed with Les Duffield, a sixty year old biker who kindly let us use his lounge floor, Geoff went off to Pete Westerman's. The following morning there was a knock at the door, Linda, in her shorty nightdress, answered it because Les had gone to work. On the doorstep was his daughter, imagine her surprise!

Linda:

We were quite a crowd leaving Perth. Me on my new R60/7 BMW, Angie and Geoff on her 350 Honda and Jacky on her 305 Honda Dream. Also some other motorcyclists from the WATC accompanied us, Trevor Thomsett, on his BMW, and another rider, with his girlfriend, on a 450 Honda.

Our first stop was to see the Karri forests in Pemberton. These giant trees grow up to 90m tall and are a type of Eucalyptus native to the wetter regions of WA. It is one of the tallest species in the world and, because of its straight trunk which only forms branches in the top third, is ideal for climbing to use as fire lookouts. The two famous trees in the area which have been preserved for this usage are the Gloucester Tree (72m) and the Diamond Tree (51m) with the original wooden platforms still in place (wa----y up the trunk). When we arrived Geoff was the only one game enough to climb them. Pemberton is a wood milling town as Karri wood, which has a mahogany appearance and is harder than pine, is used for structural building and furniture. However now pines are also planted and harvested in the area to maintain the tree stocks.

We then made our way to Albany on the southernmost part of WA where, amazingly enough, the whaling station was still in operation. Whaling was Australia's first industry. In the early 1800s British, French and American whalers were hunting in the Southern Ocean and, at the time when England was at war with France the sighting of French warships in the area caused the British to establish a permanent settlement in that part of WA. The inhabitants were quick to take up the whaling trade and work from bay whaling stations. Around 1845 whaling reached a peak all around southern Australia and most whalers were American. However, after petroleum was discovered in Pennsylvania in 1859, the demand decreased. The station in Albany was run by a Norwegian Company from 1912 but in 1916 it closed because of economic problems due to WW1. After WW2 a whaling enterprise was set up by some local salmon fishermen who did well for a while but the humpback whale was beginning to be overfished and hunting it was banned in 1963. The sperm whale had to be hunted further off shore in deeper water and this necessitated the use of a spotter plane and longer sea journeys. Finally due to economic problems and pressure from conservation groups the company closed in 1978.

When we were there we were not able to see much because the area was fenced off for work but now there is a museum on the site that fully explains the whaling industry.

It was a relatively cool and pleasant trip along the south coast to Esperance where the other motorcyclists left us as they thought our style of travel too slow. We then had to head north, inland to join the highway to Eucla on the shores of the Gt. Australian Bight. Eucla had been an important transmission station on the telegraph link from Albany to Adelaide which was set up in 1877. A small settlement was established but in the 1890s a plague of rabbits ate the vegetation that stabilized the dunes and they moved, encroaching on the town. Not able to fight the shifting sand the inhabitants moved the buildings 5km east onto higher ground but the remains of the old telegraph station are still there buried in the sand.

Just after we had been through, in 1971, there was publicity over the Nullarbor Nymph – a half naked blond woman who was supposed to run wild with the kangaroos. Having made world news and exciting many of the Australian male population, this was found to be a hoax thought up by the locals to draw tourists to the area.

And so, once more we crossed the Nullarbor, which, by the way, is not an aboriginal term, as I had always thought, but Latin, meaning 'treeless'.

As the heat had returned and although it was only in the 80s(F), I insisted that everyone took salt tablets as Mick had mentioned that he was issued them while laboring in Shark Bay, northern WA where the heat was fierce. I know that the others grumbled over my instructions and I don't know if they actually swallowed them. However, salt pills or not we survived but Jacky said it was hard to follow me as I rode too slowly. She always appeared fearless on the dirt. On the outward ride she and Angie had followed Mick blindly at his speed and not had so many spills, they learnt to keep the throttle open and hang on! With all the luggage on the bikes it was difficult, though, as the road was in bad condition after the Xmas traffic and it took us 15 hours to cover the 300 miles.

Jacky:
The highlight of the trip from Perth to Adelaide was for me the section of dirt road across the Nullarbor. I remember quite clearly travelling with Angie and Geoff and Linda following on behind. It

was starting to become dusk and Geoff said we should all travel together and as Linda was the slowest she should go first. Unfortunately, travelling behind Linda made me lose whatever skill or lack of I had and I think I came off the bike three times in about ten minutes. I recall lying in the dirt at one point and a motorist who had stopped coming up before shouting out: "It's a girl!" As it grew dark Geoff decided we should stop and so we pulled the bikes off the road, draped the tent over the handlebars and slept underneath! I was quite grateful at the time that he had sort of 'taken charge' as it felt very scary out there in the bush.

Packing up for return trip from Perth

Jacky at Albany, SW coast of WA

Dangers of the Nullarbor

Resting up after tackling the Nullarbor

Geoff, Jacky and Angie at the State Border

Well-loaded Jacky on her Honda Dream

Angie on a Trident – Southern
Cross Rally

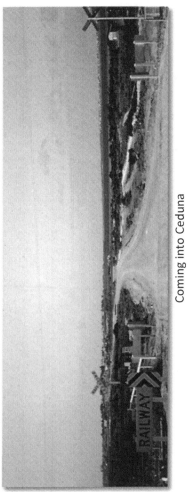

Coming into Ceduna

Are we there yet?

CHAPTER TWELVE

BACK WITH THE CROW-EATERS

<u>Linda</u>:
We arrived in Adelaide in time for the 1971 Southern Cross Rally held at Mt Barker, where we greeted our NSW and SA friends and generally had a good time. We also met Don Dobie a young PMG worker who worked in Alice Springs and Tennant creek and gave us his contact details so we would be sure to look him up when we were in the area.

I won an award for long distance solo and Angie for long distance with pillion. It was great to be back in Adelaide and we soon found a flat to use as a base while we organized our BIG TRIP. The flat was very small with one bedroom in which two single beds were squeezed. We borrowed a lazy boy as a third bed and took turns in sleeping on it.

In a block of three the construction had been cheap with flimsy walls through which we could hear the antics of the lady next door with her variety of callers. Fortunately we were not going to stay long. We all took short term jobs, myself as a driver and the others in a factory.

During this interlude Terry bussed over from Perth for a visit and made a marriage proposal which I, surprisingly, accepted. Geoff and Angie had previously decided to tie the knot so we said that we would arrange both weddings on our return – whenever that might be!

Paddy, Joe and Mick had also come over to check out the Adelaide scene and it so happened that we were all together for St Patrick's night so accompanied our Irish mates to the Celtic Club in Carrington St for the festivities. First stop the bar for a Guinness! I remember sitting on the knee of an old fella who was playing the whistle. I blew into the whistle while he did the fingering. I now know that this was old Tim Whelan- now deceased. Many years later I was to attend whistle classes in Adelaide run by Tim and learnt to play the whistle myself but I didn't know him then.

We had all knocked back quite a lot of beer and then noticed that there was a dance going on in the main hall. Paddy grabbed me as a partner and we joined in a set dance. I had never done one before and, with the beer, I was decidedly wobbly on my feet. Neither Paddy nor I knew the steps and were pushed around into place by the other dancers, laughing our heads off and messing up the whole set. More beer and then we all staggered back to the flat. It was quite a long walk and I wet myself as I was so drunk I was incapable of controlling my bursting bladder.

We all had hangovers the next day and it was a good thing that Terry had previously left for Perth and not witnessed his new fiancé in such a state!

With the other local Adelaidians, including Pete Westerman, Bob Jolly, Helen Bidstrop, Arthur Passals, Chris Witcombe, Geoff and others, fell into the habit of going to the Queens Arms in town for Saturday lunch. It was a counter meal and I always had Weiner Schnitzel for 60c. We three girls were horrified to find that, as females we were not allowed in the public bar. What!!! That is where the dart board is and, as Pommies, we were used to playing darts in the local pub. Well, with the help of our male friends we soon overcame that; as the publican could see we were serious beer drinkers he turned a blind eye. The regulars soon gave up complaining, accepted it and often joined us in a game.

We often missed any Saturday night events as we were sleeping off the afternoon sessions! However, on some of our late night exits from the pubs we would gather round one of the local pie stalls that were scattered around the city, conveniently placed for late night revelers. Something that could fill your stomach and sober you up was the ubiquitous 'pie floater'. This was a bowl of green pea soup with a meat pie floating in its centre. You could add tomato or brown sauce. There were rumours put about that certain pie stall owners thickened their soup with Plaster of Paris! Whether this was true or whether it indeed made any difference I really don't know.

Jacky :

After a disastrous couple of days in a factory counting rubber rings/bath plugs, Angie and I got jobs at Carr Fasteners where we put rivets into steel plates. This was shift work which did mean Angie got to have a go on the fork lift, one night. We travelled to work on my bike and I recall driving home one day and being stopped by the police. Women on bikes were definitely an oddity. I immediately went into a panic as the bike was registered in West Australia, my driving licence was from New South Wales and I was living and working in South Australia! I didn't have my driving licence on me, or at least I said I didn't and the police followed me home to see it. Angie and I must have had a conversation en route and what we did was to show them Angela's driving licence which was Western Australian and so at least two documents matched! We obviously didn't own up to working there.

Linda:

We were really enjoying our life in Adelaide but it was time to continue on our Big Trip. We were to go back to Sydney and then follow the east coast up as far as we could before going inland and taking the road to Darwin, then back down to Alice Springs and finally returning to our friends in Adelaide. What would happen after that we weren't sure - after all, two weddings had been planned!

Adelaide To Sydney - 1971

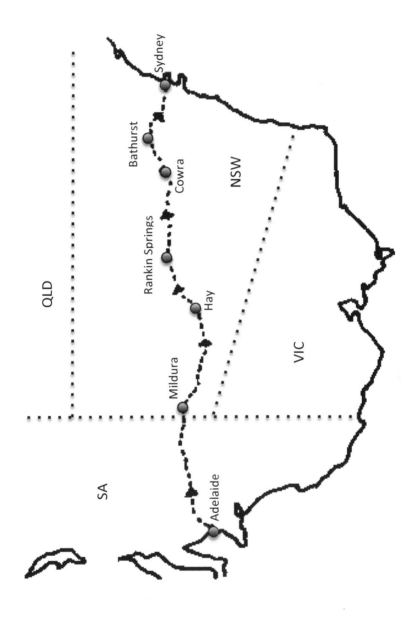

SYDNEY TO BRISBANE - 1971

CHAPTER THIRTEEN

ADELAIDE TO BRISBANE

Angie's Diaries:
7 April 1971

Left Adelaide 12.30pm Reached Mildura 5.30 averaged 60-65 mph. Did an oil change at BP station. After having our cold sausages and coffee went outside to depart to the caravan site where 2 boys came up on a Rocket 3. Were from the Mildura Wanderers Club and after talking for a bit they invited us to their club house or boathouse. There was Naked, from Queensland, on a 350 Honda. Spokes the bloke who looked after 'The Hovel' – their club house and what a hovel! A really old house. We went back then into the pub where everybody knew everybody! Then back to the Hovel with beer.

(Linda: The publican said to me that we had better watch out, being three girls among the boys, it wasn't really the sort of place we should be going to. Strange things had happened out there!)

Eventually after a singsong and discussions we adjourned to our dirty, windowless bedroom – but there was a bed each! Two boys lived there but Naked never made it so there were three. Had to find a convenient bush out the back as their plumbing was non-existent. Most embarrassing as they had the field sprinklers going and you had to time it in between as they jetted by.

(Jacky: I thought we stayed at their place cause there was no where else!! What hussies we were! I seem to remember that there was a string of ring pulls stretching from ceiling to floor.)

8 April 1971 Mildura
19592   19700   1 ½ gals

Posted Geoff's letter and left about 9.30. None of us feeling too bright, especially with the prospect of another 500 miles! Filled up in Balranald. A nice day. Warming up a bit. Reached Hay lunchtime stopped for food. Then after a warning about grasshoppers we left. For the next 100 miles to Rankin Springs we were plagued by large grasshoppers – millions of them. From all directions and at 60mph they're pretty painful. They were smashing over our face, clothes, goggles and bike. The smell was horrible. It's a seasonal happening – but the local yokels said it was especially bad.

Bloke at the Shell pump, Rankin Springs said to Jacky, "Did you come through here last year" as he recognised us! What a relief after that, no grasshoppers. Stopped before Grenfell for a hamburger. By which time it was about 5.30 and getting dark. The screw had come out in the head lamp and was rattling so I taped it. Consequently the light was bad. I was following Linda and Jacky. We went over a couple of miles of dirt and my gear lever fell off. Jacky and I got stuck behind a lorry which was throwing muck up everywhere. We stopped further up the road and I took the tape off.

On reaching Cowra I stopped Linda and said I was staying the night at Cowra. We all stayed and went to the caravan site $1.10 for the night. We only put up one tent. Had a shower – luxury and an early night. But it was so cold! My rash is back. Next morning after coffee we left loads of bikes everywhere pouring through Cowra.

9 April 1971

Jacky's plugs need replacing also a new air filter so we couldn't go over 60 mph. A nice road into Bathurst – the hills very pretty. Vegetation so different – much greener. The whole town of Bathurst was inundated with bikes. All types – bikes and riders. I felt so nervous – then shocked when at Mt Panorama (the racetrack and camp site) we were charged $3.00 to get in!!!

The track starts on the flat where the pits and start are. It then rises to some bends about the top of the track. Here you go off to the right. The camp site, which was all dirt track, wobble wobble (mainly sand and dust). Didn't know where to go – so many people. Then marvellous – Dennis came rushing over waving frantically. Salvation. We then met Steven, Lance and Jim. Then Peter Mitchell came over. He has grown a beard – suits him. We then were supposed to pay $1.00 to get in the camp site. Between the fence and the toilet block was a gap so we rode in through there – naughty. No good getting old unless you get crafty! We built a fire and all sat round it yarning (as Dennis would say).

Linda went off to see anybody she knew, with lagerphone attached to BMW. Watched the practice for about 1 hour. Sitting round fire about 7.00, now dark and very cold. Peter Hall had previously come up on the bike (still very oil-tight and a screen)

Came back with Trevor who has grown a beard. Also Richard Evans and Jeff. Exactly the same.

Linda and I then left and went into Bathurst. Although Friday, and Good Friday at that, we got in the pub round the back. There was Jim Beresford, his wife Lorraine and her father and his three children. Saw their wedding photos. She seems a very nice girl. Had a beer with them. Stan Ogden came up. Jim left. We went into the party at the back of the pub. Barry Ryan and Frank there. Talking to Stan, all about his trip to England. How he loved the place. Felt terrible I was so scruffy – hands filthy and clothes too. Needless to say no showers at the camp site. Had to quieten down a bit when the cops went in the front dining part. Left about 10.15. Going into the campsite Spokes came up and we stopped at their fire. Cliff brought his guitar out and Linda and he had a sing song, her playing the lagerphone. Went to our campsite. Ginge was awake but in his sleeping bag. Peter and Jacky were up. Peter from Melbourne we met at the Southern Cross Rally.

(Jacky: Seem to remember I fancied Peter Mitchell. Think he wanted me to go back to his place but I wasn't game for that!)

10th April 1971

Next morning after coffee we went to the edge to watch the races. The crowds! It was very hard to get to the fence. The majority seemed to be drinking, groups rolling around drunk. Jim and I got separated from the others. Found a good spot over the fence on a ride looking at the esses. There till lunchtime. Saw a sidecar turn over. No injuries and a marshall nearly collided with a side car on the bend (as if he should have even been there!) Went back to camp trying to find the others. Wrote a letter to Geoff. It had started to spit but nothing came of it. Worked our way back round.

Jim thinking quite a bit about his trip to Adelaide. Watching the bikes and who should I be standing in front of but Malcolm (Jim and Laurie fame). Has a Triumph Bonneville now. Smashed his leg and has a screw in it. Going home to England August. Bringing some photos round Monday night to Mrs Beresford's. Then Bruce came up. He has grown a moustache. It was really great to see him. Talking about Brian and old times. He's now doing dirt track racing. He said I'd lost weight!! Beam! Beam! Met the others and we went back to the camp site. Jim packed his Bultaco, Steve, Dennis and Lance left in the car. Peter Mitchell left and gave Peter (folk) a lift to Sydney. So we were left on our own. God it feels horrible when people leave.

Went into Bathurst to the pub and were talking to Malcolm. Bushey (Dave Bush) and Brian Sprawson (*Linda: These two were from the Saltbox MCC in UK and were then working on the building of the Sydney Opera House*) who had come up early in the day were in the pub. Also Doug, an American who was getting sloshed. We were having a good discussion and getting cold looks from the bartender. Stan left me his address. Then left 10.15 – all pretty well away. Having passed the camp site entrance, Bushey came in on foot got our pass and went out and brought the car in. Doug had walked in and from the pillion directed me to their campsite. They were camped on the edge in high grass. Had a few cans and Linda sang a couple of songs. We followed Greg and Kiwi friend of theirs back to our campsite. The back way – which we would not have attempted had we been sober.

11th April. 1971

Next morning not feeling too good (getting to be a habit this feeling!) We packed up. Bushey and Brian, Greg and Doug came to say goodbye. We left about 10.15 had to go on the dirt track – the back way as the road was closed for the car practice. Filled up once with petrol. Richard passed us – smug brat, blew his horn and turned round and gave one of his smiles! Did not get to Sandra's till about 2.00. Had taken us nearly 4 hours to do 130 miles to Sydney. The traffic was that bad! Cars and bikes everywhere.

The country was so green. So different to SA and WA. Still not as lush looking as Vic. Sandra was out, but Gary was home. They've a dog and 2 goldfish. We could hardly recognise the street. So many houses built up just within a year. How time flies. Talked and watched telly. Slept under the house. All attacked by mosquitoes. Jacky and Linda couldn't sleep till 4.00 chasing them round. I've 12 bites on my face. Jacky's is also covered. Linda's eyes are all swollen.

12th April 1971

Got up about 9.30. I just laid around and caught up on my diary. Jacky, Linda and Sandra are playing darts downstairs. Sorted out our luggage for Adelaide. Will be going to Mrs Beresford's this afternoon. Kathy's grown. Sandra and Gary haven't changed. She's doing very well at road racing. Says she'll come over in June to Adelaide for the wedding. Left about 4.00, filled up, rode into Burwood and into Beresford's house and they were standing there. Made us feel really welcome. Had tea. Lorraine was there. Malcolm came. Had a ride on his Triumph down to the pub.

13th April 1971

Burwood – Heard Laurie come in during the night and exclaim on sight of us, "What are they doing here?" Got up 8.30 had breakfast. They think they'll be able to make it for the wedding. Laurie was amazed to hear about Linda and me. Went to Vic Lyons Homebush to see if they could do a service. No. Jim Eade – no. So in the end Ryans did it $16.40! ugh. New seals in the points cover – cam followers. Then to John Galvin's who hasn't been seen for weeks. No extra cables for Linda. Then into town. No letters at the GPO. The traffic is diabolical and the fumes and dirt – terrible. Took us an hour to get into town!! Picked up my bike.

20344 (full tank) Got an air filter for Jacky's bike at Bennett Wood. Put it in there in their front court. Linda got a parking ticket outside Ryan's but rushed out and the copper said "Tear it up when you get round the corner (interstate plates)".

Finally settled and we were away on the highway. 20c toll charges and travelled about 2 hours in the dark. Arrived at Dennis' about 7.45pm. Mrs Hodges home. Gran now in an old people's home. Mr Hodges on late shift. Dennis left 9.30. Lance left then as well. Got to bed 12.00 absolutely shattered – fell asleep watching telly.

Oil change 1000 miles from Sydney.

14th April 1971 E. Maitland

Awoke 7.30. Mrs Hodges (an early bird) made breakfast for us. Then after chatting for a bit Jacky, Ginge and I went to a handicraft shop in E. Maitland. Dennis had brought the three of us a beautiful hand- made bag – shoulder way. Mine is black and white. The four of us went into Maitland. Jacky's back tyre was down put a valve in it, spare one I had. Seems alright. Got new pair goggles. New hair brush. Card for Charlie's birthday. Drew out $10 must keep a rough account of where it goes. Came back had lunch. Linda and Jacky doing an oil change. I'll fill up Cathery? Clean bike a bit – looks much better. Drew out $10.00. Had tea. Steve came round brought some beer. Watched late movie.

15th April 1971 East Maitland

10.30 Left Maitland

20457 20582 83c

125 1 ¾ gals

Taree

20700 Kempsey

Left Dennis just outside Maitland – Raymond Terrace. Pacific Highway to Bulahdelah. Turned east towards the ocean along Ocean Drive – really lovely. All these lakes and at parts the ocean on the other side. Very green and lush. Went to Wallingna N.P. and saw the forest (fig trees oldest one 1600 years old) Loads of vines and creepers round the trees made it look very tropical. Then into Forster where on turning down wrong road, Linda and I slowed down. Jacky couldn't stop and as I pulled to the left I hit her alongside and she then veered and clipped Linda. This brought the two of them down. Jacky hurt her foot. Linda knocked a lump off the right pot. Jacky's already got a bruised hand.

Forster's quite pretty. It's all so commercialised, typically tourist! Taree had hamburger at BP. On to Port Macquarie. Very clean all laid out. Museum didn't open till 5.00 so with only 10 mins to go went to Fantasy Glades 40c. Very bad – a real take. 2 midgets, 2 houses small ones – actually it was like a children's playground. Then onto Kempsey – couldn't get into the campsite – full. Cop told me to, "Put your lights on!" Then J and L "Get off the road". Just cos we were doing a uey! (U-turn) Did not have to be rude!! Camped 50c each.

$2 Petrol .40 Glade .50 camp 1.20 food Total $4.10

16th April 1971 Kempsey

20700

20776 1 gal Coffs Harbour 50

20895 1 ½ 83

20944 ¾ Byron Bay 39

Left Kempsey 10.30 (getting later and later) Made Coffs Harbour by 12.30 pm. Where we stopped in the High Street waiting for Jacky who had been caught up in the traffic. Whereupon we were surrounded by men appearing from nowhere. Linda being the friendliest they circled her bike while Jacky and I poured over the tourism of Coffs Harbour. Namely the "biggest banana in the world." After pies we left.

The road (Pacific Highway) from Kempsey till now is terrible. There are ridges everywhere holes and dips you had to keep your eyes on the road condition all the time. We reached 'The Big Banana'. It's concrete constructed with pics inside of banana production. A banana plantation (bananas before they are ready for picking need 18 months!!!) They had a gift shop and café also I brought an ashtray for $3.50, it is made of port wood. Rather nice. Took some photos of big banana.

(Linda: There were chocolate-coated frozen bananas on sticks – very yummy.)

Then carried on to Grafton. Scenery is very much like Victoria. Quite green and beautiful. The rivers of which there are plenty are all terribly wide. Parts reminding us all of the Thames. Peculiar creek names such as Scrubby Creek, Frying Pan Creek, Boot-Booti Creek, Man arm Creek. Withdrew $60 from Grafton as I thought they'd retain my bank book but didn't. Decided to stop at Byron Bay the most easterly part of Australia. Two miles off highway. Very pretty hilly country road. Filled up, camped had banana sandwiches and then down to the pub for a few beers - in bed by 9.30 pm! Started to rain and so madly brought gear in. Spent £2.00 petrol $3.50 ashtray 0.53 camp $1.00 beer 0.47 food – TOTAL $7.50

17ᵗʰ April 1971

20944 109 1 ¾

21155 102 1 ¾ 92

Left the campsite my bike only firing properly on one side. Here we go! Went along the coast road to the lighthouse. At the lighthouse I wiped some oil off the plugs. It's a very pretty lighthouse built 1901. Byron Bay is the most easterly point of Australia. Left there. Bike still missing. Stopped. Changed plugs. Tried without new cap. Cleaned float bowl, blew down jets. Manicured points. Tried Linda's spark plug. All to no avail!! Got out onto the Pacific Highway. The missing went and we cruised along at 60.

Got to Coolangatta and Tweed Heads. Took photos. Had pie and back on the road. By-passed Brisbane and through Ipswich out to Toowoomba. Went onto reserve filled up 28 miles out. By this time it was raining heavily. Donned wet gear. Got into Toowoomba about 5.00 asked at a couple of garages about the TMC Club. Then the cop shop – no luck. Not a single bike in town. Discovered petrol leaking from the float bowl. Toowoomba is quite a large town we were very surprised it's called "Garden City of Brisbane". It's in the Great Dividing Range – consequently the horrible weather!

Then we went through Surfers Paradise – Golden Mile – So holiday-ish – swimming pools – all big buildings with flats. It was as if everybody was on holiday. The weather – holiday weather as well cos once we started to come away, admittedly it was inland, it started raining. None of us liked it anyway. At the garage petrol leaking – pouring out! Getting dark - bike wouldn't start. Jacky and Linda went off to pitch the tents. I started to dismantle the carby and this boy on a Kawasaki had stopped and was watching as I took the bowl off and looked down. He touched the floats, which then fell off losing the pin and jet into the bike. Found the jet after wheeling and shaking the bike the pin fell out, after putting it together it still leaks. Left it in the garage. Went into town met bloke who went to SCR had a few beers met all the local idiots brought a keg and went back to one of their flats. Left about 10.00. Slept well. It's still raining. $2.09 petrol .63 food .50 beer .50 campsite TOTAL 3.63

18th April Toowoomba

21155

Started on my Honda. It's pouring. After cleaning, wiping mantling and dismantling the carby we eventually stopped it from leaking. We weren't aware of what we'd done still it worked. Started it up excitedly. Still missing on the left side. Air lined the carby jets. Checked plugs, points. Can't do nothing else so left it in the garage. Went into town for food. Then up to Picnic Point. What a crummy place this is. Dead. Sat up there. Quite a nice scene. Pulling peoples dress to verbal shreds. Then to the Cobb & Co Museum. All the old coaches and relics. Very interesting. We were the only ones there. Then onto the Lionel Lindsay Art Gallery. All his work plus his brother's. Daryl being the youngest and is still alive. Kicked out at 5.00 and back to the campsite. Didn't fancy the session. Campsite Linda practised her banjo and brought children round. Jacky played snap with me. Retired to Linda's tent with biscuits and cards. Fellow camper details about floods still north. Ugh! .30 Museum .40 camp 1.50 rod Total $2.20

19th April 1971 Toowoomba

Monday morning rode the 80 miles to Brisbane after taking my bike into the Honda Agent who being two old boys of retirement age rabbited on, not seeming to know what they were talking about. Took the Honda into Bennett-Honda and left it there for a general perusal. Brisbane is quite pretty. Lots of bridges as it's off the coast and on the Brisbane River. Story Bridge unusual.

The houses in Queensland are nearly all built of wood. They stand on stilts. This is so the air can circulate more freely. As it's such a humid climate that after tropical rain downpours the brick wouldn't dry out. Learnt from an inhabitant that this was the reason for a lot of the people's colds who lived in brick houses.

Went to see Angela's mother. Angela is a girl Linda met on the ship coming out here. Went to pick my bike up and was told that the piston had gone on the left as the compression was nearly half that of the right side, also the cam chain. Terribly upset and worried thinking of the damage to the rest of the engine. We then went off to find Geoff Howie's flat. Dark and we eventually found it. Linda met him at Bathurst last year. He lives with his girlfriend Karen. Bruce and Frank – brothers. They said we were welcome to stay.

Mt Panorama, Bathurst with Sydney boys

A coastal port, NSW

Leaving Ginge's house, East Maitland

One of many Scrubby Creeks

BRISBANE TO CAIRNS - 1971

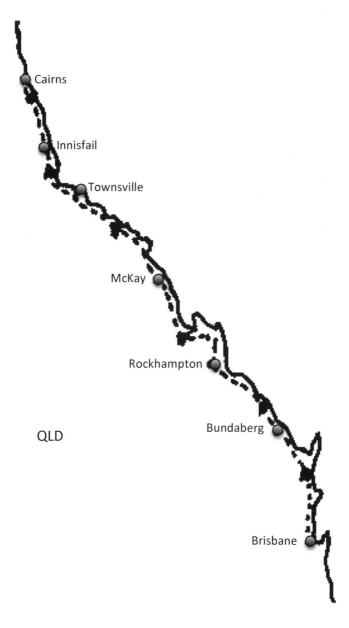

Cairns

Innisfail

Townsville

McKay

Rockhampton

QLD

Bundaberg

Brisbane

Chapter Fourteen

Brisbane to Cairns

Angie's diaries:

20th April 1971 Brisbane – Northgate

Geoff and Karen suggested I take the bike to Peter Gleeson as he was good and a friend of theirs and Bennett-Hondas were useless. I refused to ride the bike over there and so after describing to Peter the problem he didn't see how the piston could have gone, judging by the symptoms. He said check the oil, see if there were any bits of metal. Back through town once again (Karen was on holiday, lucky for me, and was showing us the way). Found a piece semi-circular and little bits, not much. Took the risk and rode it over. Peter looked at it and said the cam shaft was loose and flapping about, could already have done damage and was likely to do more. Much relieved, I took the bike back to Northgate, crying out of self pity and for my poor bike, which although was bad still kept going for me.

(Linda - It was now that we decided that Angie's bike probably needed a lot of time and money spent on it and the best thing we could do was send it back to Adelaide by train where Geoff and the others could sort it out. Angie would come pillion with me on the BMW. This meant that we would have to drastically cut down on our luggage and would send a lot back to Adelaide with the bike.)

Sorted out our gear. Now down to one tent, no radio, 2 pairs trousers, we managed to get everything on the two bikes. Jacky cutting down on her stuff. Loaded the Honda up and back into town. We eventually found the goods station in South Brisbane and after packing the bike with the returned gear it was put in the shed ready for departure then next day. This took us till 5.30 pm. What a tiring day. We then got caught in the traffic. Had stew (Karen's concoction) pineapple and ice cream. Nice to have a decent meal. About 8.15 pm Linda and I went out to Sunnybank to see Angela, the girl Linda knew on the ship. She arrived home and married a school teacher whom she'd known before. Very nice couple. He was a typical school teacher. Sunnybank was some miles out of Brisbane and we felt the cold as we got further out in the bush. Got back about 1.00am.

21st April 1971 Northgate

10903 (speedo reading on Linda's BMW)

Karen took us out to Lone Pine Koala Sanctuary. It was 60c to get in you could only hold the koalas if the official cameraman took a photo of you at an extremely unreasonable price of over a dollar. Photo of an albino koala. There were emus, deer and kangaroos and wallabies loose in an enclosure which you were allowed to walk around and feed. All took photos. They had cockatoos, pea fowl, guinea pigs, doves, Tasmanian Devils, dingos, snakes, possums. Bought another film.

Went into Brisbane then got Jacky's plugs that morning. Had something to eat at Coles. Brought some postcards, Linda got her spoon. Then back to Northgate. Managed to pack everything up and we left about 4.00 pm. Got cold pretty quick stopped at a caravan park near the Ginger Factory and Pioneer Cottage which we are going to see tomorrow. Had biscuits and coffee. Did 64 miles. Passed the Glasshouse Mts stand straight out from the ground, very irregular shaped.

(*Jacky: I remember when we first got to Brisbane it was lunchtime and for some reason, unlike us, we decided to have a 'counter lunch'. They refused to serve us in the bar we were in and said we weren't allowed in the bar that they did serve lunch in because we were female. Not sure if I have got this right but seem to remember we got kicked out. I also remember the koala sanctuary and thinking "this was what I came here for!!!!" Just the memory of the picture of the koala as a kid kicked in.*)

22nd April 1971 Nambour Qld

10967 $40 Sketch of old rocking horse

Buderim

Left about 10.00 went too far back towards Brisbane. Arrived at the Ginger Factory Buderim about 11.00 where we watched a film on the production of ginger. This being the only ginger factory in the Southern Hemisphere. We were given pamphlets and then went upstairs to see the ginger production. It's the rhizome of the ginger plant which is harvested in March when the plant hasn't reached full maturity so it's not too hot or fibrous. This is harvested by hand. The other is cropped May to August mainly for drying dehydrating used for spices, soft drinks. This crop is harvested by hand. Only grown in an area of 35 miles around Buderim. They store the roots in brine vats so giving all year round work for employees. Used to grow coffee until the 2nd World War but couldn't get the labour. Looked in the factory and saw the girls cutting up the roots by hand.

Then at about 11.30 am we went to the Pioneer Cottage up the road. Built in 1876 by John Burnett one of Buderim's earliest homes. Built mainly of cedar. Very interesting. Got kicked out at 12.30 pm just not long enough to see everything. Then after pie and apple we went back to the Ginger Factory 'Merrybud' where Jacky and I sent some chrystalised ginger home to Mum.

From there carried on the Bruce Highway then off to Tewantin where we walked round the bottle house. Home composed of bottles cemented in. Thousands of different types of bottles. Purple bottles which having laid in the sun eventually absorbed the permanent colour given off by the ultra violet rays of the sun. A very attractive stubby shaped bottle made of bottles with a spiral staircase and beautiful displays of oriental large and colourful bottles on the way. Then a slide on the outside of the stubby.

Bought a gourd. It's a large pod with seeds in it. Bottle shaped. Was used as a water carrier. Will varnish it; looks very unusual cost 30c. Linda brought one as well. Another 20c to see the sand display too much my boy!!! Then up to Gympie where we had coffee then 50 miles east to Rainbow Beach. But as the coloured sands are a six mile walk away we've decided against bothering to see them. In a fairly small area of beach there are various different colours of sands ranging from pure white to black, a range of yellows, reds, brown, beiges, in- between. Some dispute with the authorities as firms are interested in the phenomena with possible mineral qualities. The people however want to keep it as so. You are not permitted to remove the sand (ho ho). They charge in the region of 50c for a small and I mean small bottle of mixed sands! Cashing in!

Camped for the night 27c each. Bore water for washing looks a light brown and tank water for drinking. There's a room with telly, table and chairs so we're all busy tonight. Washed my hair.

.27 camp .75 food 1.20 ginger factory .20 Pioneer Cottage .60 Bottle Shop Total $3.02

23rd April 1971 Rainbow Beach

11128 255 miles

Got into Gympie and it started to rain. Saw this old car and boy do I mean old – hand painted and rough! Had a red painted bucket on the running board - on closer observation there was the driver. An old man sitting bolt upright clasping the wheel and staring straight ahead. All wheels wobbling, no indicators! A real character.

We all put on our waterproofs, well, hardly waterproof, but an offering. Stopped at Maryborough while the rain continued to pour and pour. We sat inside an Ampol garage and ate and ate. Then I put Linda's space blanket over the sleeping bags on the back of Jacky's bike which were by then quite wet but not through and I rode Jacky's bike till we reached Miriam Vale where we stopped and went to the campsite. For the last hour of sunlight we hung our bags and wet lilos up. Six o'clock we were down the pub. Bought some sandwiches and then a round each by which time we were chatting to the people in the lounge and the drinks were just coming from nowhere. Talking to this bloke called Lindsay who gave us the names of some pubs in Ingham north of Townsville where we might get a job if we got stranded due to the weather. RAIN!

We were warned in no uncertain terms about a stretch of road under repair which was pretty treacherous. Needless to say immediate panic! Had a very good birthday night there. Linda ended up singing and doing a jig. Left about 10.30 and all fell into bed. None of us feeling the damp bedding. .34 camp .50 beer 1.20 food Got up at 5.00 all of us being sick and very thirsty.

24th April 1971 Miriam Vale

11383 160 miles

All had hangovers and kept drinking. Eventually we packed the tent and made off about 11.30. The BMW without me but with the tent and rest of the rubbish. We were very lucky as the sun that morning had baked the road dry so it was just holey. We could just imagine it yesterday as it was clayey mud and would have been like ice when wet.

Arrived in Rockhampton. Took photos of the Tropic of Capricorn which we passed through. Too late for the tour of the Mount Morgan open cut mine for gold and copper. Going to try tomorrow. Rockhampton is quite pretty, situated on the Fitzroy River we've camped on the river bank opposite the town. Lots of horse riders in Queensland steering the cattle in. Not much of the farmland is fenced off consequently there are cattle roaming the roads – which we came across quite often and quite unexpected! A kangaroo leapt off the side of the road into the bush the other day. Still can't get used to seeing Queensland reg. plates.

25th April 1971 Rockhampton

11543 120 miles

Left this morning for the Mt Morgan mine. Arrived about 9.15 and were the only ones on the tour. The guide was very nice and helpful. He gave us some metal in the rock. We walked up the side of the mountain. A mountain which was made up from what they've scooped out from the inside mining in the open cut manner and lodged all round in large rocky slag heaps. A stack built by the first company that owned the mine stands to the height of the original mountain – what a difference now!!!

Mount Morgan is purely a mining village which was practically non-existent during the depression as the mine was hardly working. They hope to be able to continue mining profitably for another twelve years - after – goodness knows what happens. They'll be 900 at least out of work. Where the rocks are broken down and smelted the sulphur fumes are given off and boy do they smell! The turnover of employees in that section is in the hundreds. The heat is also tremendous. We were shown the mine from the top – it's the deepest open cut mine in the southern hemisphere. Saw the crushing of it and then it's mixed with about six different chemicals. The high and low grades are being separated. Its then passed on and dried off after going through a dam – cement tank and once dried it falls down into the trucks. From there it's smelted in the furnaces 310 degrees and results in bars a mixture of copper, gold and silver. Some gypsum is also extracted for use in cement. The bars are sent to Japan where they are electrically separated. They used to do it in NSW.

From there we went into the town and had a hamburger. There were Anzac Parades in the town – or had been. Went round via the dam up on wrong dirt road, catastrophe. Then back through town and over the Fitzroy River to the Commo Caves. Another dirt road. Linda kept saying: "God, I hope it doesn't rain while we're inside." It was muddy. We discovered that the caves were $1.00 to see. Disgusting! Jacky and I decided against it as caves aren't particularly our line and for that price it most certainly isn't!! The people that run it were most put out that we didn't do the tour. Money-grabbing......! Linda went in and said it was bad. A dry cave.

Left there and went to the Botanical Gardens. Scottish Band were playing. Some impressive fernery. All the plants getting tropical now.

From the south side of town we went back to the north side and climbed Mount Archer. A beautiful view of the town, although it was misty. There were volcanic eruptions and it was dusk and a lot of water in the area. It looked quite eerie. Stopped at the fish and chip shop and went next door for a beer. A drunken ex-soldier brought us another round. Anzac day and all that!

26th April 1971 Rockhampton

11663 309 mls

Countryside very green and lush. Left about 9.30 am came across a lot of unmade roads. Also a one track road predominated. Either side being thick mud. Luckily on such roads the cars nearly always give way to us and go half off the road. Jacky was in front and a pot hole covered ¾ of the road, she was unable to go round it as there was a car coming the other way so she went through it and so did we, the impact immediately opened the top box lid and it flew open and hit me in the back and scattered a few things across the road. Linda stopped and I went back and got them off the road and off we went.

The roads are very bad. About 25 miles up the road Linda remembered something else from the box which we hadn't retrieved. So Jacky went on and we went back. Unable to find it. The BMW manual and some letters. We caught Jacky up as her gigantic load had fallen off all along the road. We reached Marlborough and stopped for a hamburger and coffee. Filled up. They had 'Sheik of Scrubby Creek' (Chad Morgan) playing on the juke box. Then assuming we'd fill up at Road Junction which turned out to be literally a junction no more. Jacky just limped into the Mobil Station 7 miles outside she'd cut her speed right down to conserve petrol. There was a boy on a Honda 450 who had been following us for some miles back till we'd slowed down.

Back onto the road. The sides being fenced with fields of sugar cane. One campsite a cinder ground – no good $1.40. Then said didn't want any more campers in another. Then at the Pioneer $1.20. Have to put a $2.00 deposit on the keys – mad. Off to see Penny Lawson – friend of Sandra's. A very nice couple.

$1.35 petrol $1.40 food .20 camp TOTAL $2.95

27th April 1970

11972 186 miles

Linda discovered this morning that can of oil had leaked all in the top box along with the washing up liquid. Oil everywhere. Walked down the bakery and had some buns. Going to see the natural harbour and sugar cane storage largest in the Southern Hemisphere. Quite a pretty town, trees and plants down the high street. Went to a petrol station Kaludra. Jacky filled up. Met two boys from Perth travelling in a car working round. Going to work in Cairns. Had been working and travelling for a year.

Reached Proserpine went east to the coast for about 10 miles. Found a dirt track with a gorgeous creek which had the road running through it. So I took my shoes off and paddled through it. Looking down, it's so tropical looking. Tall pines. Then Jacky stayed there and we ventured along the stony track to the Cedar Creek Falls, where the creek fell quite a drop and beneath was a natural pool. A NSW couple were swimming. After a photo we went onto the beach Conway Beach. Not very nice – could see the start of the Whitsunday Isles. A bit bleak looking.

Left there and made our way to Bowen, here we camped at Harbour Lights which looks out onto the sea. It's very nice, was $1.50. Has a laundry (free machines) a swimming pool and a free TV lounge. Never been to a better one before. We were amazed at the price. Went into town had steak-burger and hamburger and egg. Now doing the washing. Watched the free telly till 11.00 saw Steptoe and Son and, would you believe, an extremely funny Aussie panel game!

28th April 1970 Bowen

12158

Woke up sweating, felt sick and had a guts ache. Henceforth felt bad for the rest of the morning. Jacky and Linda had a swim and we left about 11.15. Went into the BP and there two boys on Yam trial 250 bikes came in. Come from Port Hedland round and were making their way to Melbourne for an interview for emigrating to Canada. They said the road from Townsville to Mt Isa was terrible (the dirt anyway!) The mud was packed solid and has gone into ridges and large pot holes where the trucks were bogged down and hauled out! All a bit dubious about it. They said after doing that trip you'd be able to do anything. Can't see that after all the trouble Richard Evans & Co had from Perth north to Darwin!!

Got into Townsville that afternoon. Went to the GPO. Walking along the street and Greg and Robin called out – they'd got there the day before. They're two boys we met on the road from Perth. Camped. Got changed and actually put dresses and make up on. Felt like girls again. Brought some beers and went to their motel room and watched telly. They (would you believe, were Aussies and not wed to beer!) were astounded by the quantities we drank. We weren't drunk but they were reeling all over the place.

29th April 1970

None of us felt bad and who should turn up but the two boys. We went into town did a bit of shopping went to the bank. Then went along to see the gem museum. This advertised in the tourist booklet. Laugh – he came out and said it wasn't for the public, he only sold them. So off we went to Castle Hill lookout – a very good view. Then to the beach. Bitten by sand-flies and so we went to the swimming pool. Here after an hour or so we were attacked by some German sailors who threw us in and they were massive blokes and we didn't stand a chance. It was then a battle at keeping above the water. Asked us what bar we drank at as we were leaving and I said we didn't drink.

(Jacky: I remember having a whale of a time with these sailors and feeling quite cheated that Angie had put them off us meeting them that night! I wasn't engaged!!! I recall also that they were Russian/Eastern European – I have some German so would have picked up on that! Also believe we couldn't swim on the beach cause of jellyfish.)

There's a beautiful waterfall right on the Strand which is the beach promenade. Bought a hamburger and then back to the camp. We went to see a drive- in at Marline $1.00. Left the bikes at the back and sat on the café patio – loud speakers. The War Wagon and Texas Across the River.

30TH April 1971

Got the boat at 9.30 for Magnetic Island 70c return. Got the bus 80c around the Island. Saw the fish and coral display – what water life (the colours). Then to the Arcadia Beach. Here the sea is enclosed with a fence to prevent stingers of sharks the mainstay of Queensland beaches, from entering. Lovely clear water. Went swimming for the afternoon. Found a dead turtle, swarming with maggots and flies. Had a few beers and then caught the bus back to the ferry. Caught the ferry and after hamburger and washed my hair we played cards with a middle-aged couple in their van.

1st May 1971 Townsville

12339 241 miles

Went to the GPO. Then carried onto Ingham where we filled up then onto Innisfail. The roads are very rough. Huge holes and gravel. Passed another motorcyclist from Vic, "Death before Dishonour" written on the back of leather jacket. After a miserable egg-burger we carried on to Cairns. After passing this motor cyclist Linda declared it was a girl! On a Kawasaki 500!

Cairns we were all rather disappointed with. It's so quiet! Although it's a Saturday afternoon it is the beginning of a bank holiday – yes another one! The third in a row. We stopped in the high street and the girl on the Kawasaki came up and spoke. Came all on her own from Ballarat. Been riding for a year. Quite a case. No gloves or scarf on her face! Very burnt! She was off to find a friend. We came to the council site $1.10 and there we met Frank and Rheen, the couple from the site in Townsville. Camping at the same site. We saw Ryan's Daughter – very good. $1.30 petrol .77 camp $1.00 food

2nd May 1971 Cairns

12580

Went up the coast about 25 miles into Hartleys Creek Zoo. Large crocs and black (rare) dingo. They look so friendly, dingoes. The exact opposite to what they are. Then a few miles up to Pebbly Beach where we sunbathed (I baked my front). Collected a few colourful pebbles and hurried back to Cairns to catch the 2.15 train to Kuranda. This is a tourist train and goes slowly along the Barron Gorge which is very striking – some falls 150ft. Stoney Creek. There's a hydro station there. The train goes round the very edge of the gorge with fantastic sheer drops, everyone was sitting on one side of the train watching the view. Had scones and coffee at the quaint plant covered railway station at Kuranda, then back on the train to Cairns.

Sunday night we had a few beers with Colin and John and Robert from the tents opposite. Nice to talk and discuss things with English and European intelligent men.

3rd May 1971

We got to the harbour at 8.00 am and brought our tickets for Green Island. Plus the entrance for the glass bottom boat. The boat was slow and took 1 ½ hours. Linda had started to feel sick by the time we got there. It's a small island 32 acres. Composed of washed up coral. Therefore is sand covered with bush trees – none of the lush greenery of the main-land.

We walked to the theatre and booked for the 2.00 performance.

Then we went into the Marine Land. Nothing marvellous. Saw some stingrays. A lot of the pens empty. Then walked along the footpaths round the island – which only takes a few minutes. Back to the motel, the only one there, with exorbitant prices. Ate our bread and butter then lay on the beach for an hour. I kept covered apart from my legs as I'm still burnt.

Went on the boat inspection. Fascinating. The glass enables you to see the life underneath. Fantastic place for ski or scuba diving. Then a couple of beers with Frank and Rheen and saw the theatre. Very good film by Noel Monkman who does a lot of research on the island. Jacky bought me a book on the coral and slides for my birthday. Caught the boat after a beer at 3.30pm. Arrived at Cairns 4.45pm. A message from Greg and Robin so they came to the site and we went out for a drink with them. They had got jobs. Celebrated our 2 years freedom! *(Linda: This was connected with the immigration policy, that we had to stay two years or pay our outward fare back.)* Got back to the campsite and had a beer with Colin and John and R.

4th May 1971

This was maintenance day. Jacky and I went into town to the GPO. What a lovely surprise I had there. Then we ambled round the shops. Tried to get some canvas bags as mine are badly ripped. No luck I brought a carved coconut head. Also a moss agate. I managed to get for half the price!!! Went into Rusty Reece's Cycle Shop at 11.30. There we found Linda so Jacky took her bike round the back did an oil change, took a couple of links out of the very slack chain. Linda did a complete engine oil change and fork change. We were there till about 4.00. Then we walked round the shops – had our tea then left about 5.00 back to the camp.

Later on that evening John and Colin went out and brought some beer, we gave them $1.00 each. (Robert had been invited out to dinner by a Swedish woman) We sat there till about 1.00 drinking discussing and laughing. No doubt the whole campsite could hear!!! What conversations!! After John and Jacky went out for hamburgers we all then hit the sack.

(Linda- We did not go any further north than Cairns as the roads were all unsealed and too bad for us. We planned to return to Townsville where we could take the inland road through Mt Isa to the Centre.)

With Karen at Wildlife Park

Ginger factory at Buderim, QLD

A wishing well

Packed up for three on two bikes

Linda and Jacky at the
Tropic of Capricorn

Green Island, Qld

Railway from Cairns to Kuranda

CAIRNS TO DARWIN - 1971

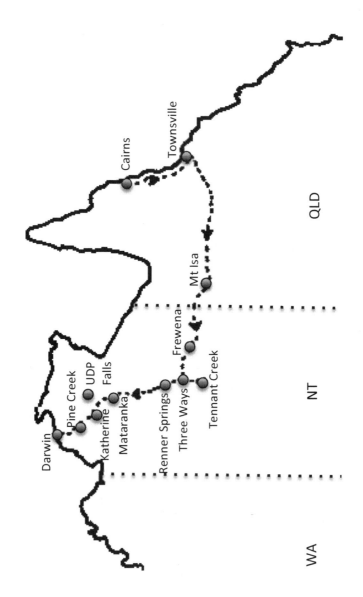

CHAPTER FIFTEEN

CAIRNS TO MATARANKA

Angie's Diaries:
5th May 1971 Cairns
    12666 132 miles

Colin and John went to work. We eventually got up and packed, leaving 10.30. Said goodbye to Robert. Frank and Rheen had said goodbye and left for Cooktown. We have now a lot more stuff to pack. Consequently I am holding a Pacific bag full. *(Jacky: Plastic bags Linda had purloined from her previous employer)*. Made our way to the Atherton Tableland. Huge red anthills everywhere. The vegetation changed very quickly back to typical bush black boys (Yuccas or Xanthorrhoea) once we were a few miles inland. Stopped at a honey house. Very amusing, whisky labels and rum etc. on honey bottles. Then to Lake Fitan which holds three quarters the amount of Sydney Harbour. Irrigates this area of tobacco fields. Then to Lake Eachan. Very peaceful, pretty. We tried to catch the small fish with our hands and Linda's scarf. A few small turtles there as well. Suddenly there descended loads of children (teenagers) so we left, the peace shattered. Camped at Malanda Falls and swimming pool here, beautiful. Then went to the crater. Found it in some tropical forest. As Linda said, "You'd expect to see Tarzan leaping about". Huge vines and thick forest. The crater was very eerie. Holds two hundred feet of water. It's an extinct volcano. Sheer steep sided drop. Beautiful continuing rapids called the Dinner Falls. Nearly dark so we made our way back to camp. Had big nosh up – sausage sarnies. Early to bed.

    6th May 1971 Malanda
    12798

Froze last night. Not surprising as we're over 3,000 ft above sea level! I went in for a swim in the creek swimming pool – boy oh boy was it cold . But so exhilarating. It smelt like the River Thames and the stream where we used to catch tadpoles! Nobody there. Suddenly coach full of teenagers so I was out! Left after 11.00. Stopped at

Malanda and brought some cards. Huge anthills after Cairns on the tablelands. Then went to some falls at Millaa Millaa. Then to the Zillie Falls. This was along the dirt track. It was quite bad actually very gravelly. Jacky and Linda felt quite exhausted. The countryside reminded us of Wales and but for the constant sunshine it could easily have been!

We got back onto the highway, joke, the condition of the roads are terrible. Gravel strewn across, very dangerous on unexpected corners! Went through tropical forests flanking either side of the road. Large, looming, dark green trees and vines, palms and an eerie silence classic to such vegetation areas. The trucks come roaring round the corners and cars pulling vans giving us quite a turn.

Reached Innisfail about 1.45 pm decided on a counter lunch after just savouring it we were told it was too late and off! Carried on till Cardwell and had a steakburger. Left there and reached Townsville couldn't get in at Raves Bay C/P so off we went to another one. Met the bikies on the campsite. One, Ron Tiemstre owns a white BMW 750 new. Couple of blokes with Honda 350 cc. Ron let us have our tea in his caravan. Lives here with his brother.

7th May 1971 Townsville

Went into town and got my post. We walked round the town looking at the shops. I bought a kangaroo paw bottle opener on a discount $5.35. Postcards. Came back to the campsite did the washing. Washed both bikes. Washed my hair. Had our tea in Ron's van and Jacky and Linda went out for some beers. Ron's a real unusual character, really funny – not like a BMW owner. Terrible night's sleep. The floor felt so hard.

8th May 1971 Townsville

Jacky and Linda keen on the idea of working in the prawn factory for a week. I don't fancy the idea but anyway following the majority we went off to Mt Spec with Ron. "That turns me on!" We stopped at some falls on the way up the 2 miles of windy road (and I mean windy!) Ron swam, we watched. At the top we had scones, jam and butter just from the oven! Beautiful! Then back down and we swam apart from Jacky, and I had a go with Ron's goggles and snorkel. After we went on the highway and stopped at Rollinstone Creek. Swam again. Saw all these fishes! "Christmas!" Lost the metal clamp round the goggles – sorry Ron. Got back and we all felt exhausted.

No-one's keen on the prawn idea now – thank goodness. Had

curry and rice, banana and ice cream – what luxury!! Back in Ron's van – says he doesn't know what he'll do when we go! Got the name and address of some of his friends at Mt Isa.

9th May 1971 Townsville

Left 10.30 with Ron getting 'melabolic' raving on how we should get up earlier! What a character. Filled up a few miles out and said farewell to Ron. Picked up some string on the way, side of the road. Passed a yellow Monaro who proceeded to follow us. When Jacky lost the water bottle – they picked it up. At Charters Towers they stopped for petrol like us. Tried to chat us up. A few miles later they picked up two dolly hitchhikers so they weren't interested anymore – thank god. At Pentland all we could find were the loos. So had a pie each at Torrens Creek. Jacky's and Linda's being stone cold. Reached Hughenden about 4.00pm. No caretaker so we got out then had a few beers, a terrible hamburger and heard all about the dirt to Cloncurry from a girl who'd just put her car and self on the train over.

10th May 1971 Hughenden

13470 265 miles

After our early night 8.30 pm would you believe! We got up just before 7.00am I had shoo-ed a dog away during the night and we'd all frozen. Such extremes of temperature . Filled up with petrol roped all the gear on Jacky's bike down and were on our way by 8.15 am. Ron would have been proud of us!! All wondering what the dirt had in store for us. After the tales of bogged cars, ruts and water!

The first section of dirt was very good – hard with a slight loose top. Jacky led the way, as she did through it all. We had a good steady speed between 50-60 mph and got to Richmond 9.50 am. Jacky drew out some money and after filling up with petrol we set off for Julia Creek. Had a good run of bitumen for about 30 miles and then dirt. This section wasn't as good as the last getting more mud packed ridges which the cars and trucks had made while it was still wet.

The country is much drier, although the vegetation is greener than parts of SA and WA. A lot of sheep now, dead on the road by cars or at the sides. Often hawks or eagles flying away from the corpses – if not- then zooming and hovering in the sky, quite eerie. A snake slithered by and Linda ran over its tail, she didn't see it as she was concentrating on the road so much! Not a lot of traffic on this road.

Stopped at Julia Creek and had a pie each, now .25c as opposed to 16c!! There's a few stretches of bitumen which suddenly appear over a creek. This I decided must be done due to the creek flooding and keeps the road in a better condition there as they can't afford to do the whole road. This puts you in a fools' paradise till you hit the dirt again. This last stretch started about a mile out of Julia Creek.

Continued for over 50 miles. This was indeed the worst stretch! Our speed was down by at least 10mph and very much less in parts. Jacky went boring through everything. Linda kept up and was quick and fairly confident. Came to three pigs running along the highway. Saw this muddy wet dip in the road. A tractor was there and he told us to go round we started to plough towards this ditch and he was frantically waving his arms and told us to go round the town which was to the right so sigh of relief and round we went.

A few corrugations, holes and ridges. Came to a wet creek, where a lorry had got bogged with half its load. He told Jacky to go round to the side which wasn't so deep. Also would she tell the grader they were bogged. I got off and walked over the stones and took photos for everyone. Further on we came to a worse creek. Much fuller and steeper sides. A road man was there so Jacky informed him of the lorry's plight. I took my shoes and socks off and helped Linda through. It was very muddy and we feared the engine might stop and fill with water. Then Jacky once she was in the water she opened the throttle and got through. I took photos from the other side and thought it was a great laugh. I was thoroughly enjoying myself. Jacky had a very close one. Falling first one way – opened the throttle- then fell to the other side – opened the throttle – and righted herself and ran it into a mud ridge to stop herself as she had no brakes! Couple of times I leapt off in dodgy parts. Saw a herd of goats.

We have seen four Scrubby Creeks to-date. Not as dusty as the Nullarbor, but the last stretch of about 20 miles was very much like the Nullarbor. More dust, quite loose gravel and flat. No more dips or creeks or bends. Got onto a patch of bitumen and Linda sighed and said, "Think I'll get off and kiss the ground." A couple of miles further we went back onto dirt. Going west as well and the sun was beginning to sink lower and get in our eyes. Reached Cloncurry and decided to stay at the camp site. Now in a café having an after dirt celebration meal of bacon and eggs!!!

11th May 1971 Cloncurry

13735 105 miles

Left about 8.30am. Very cold and windy for the 75 miles to Mt Isa. Beautiful rugged countryside. Rocks, anthills, eagles, caves. Dark red-brown dirt. Typical cowboy countryside. Linda had a new back tyre $12 and $2 for putting it on! ½ hours work by a kid! Then walk round the town, eat and in for the tour of the mine. Safety glasses, dust coats, helmets. Too late to go in the normal bus, so went with the Central Tours coach with a load of young silly Aussies (what a scream that was). Not as good as the Mt Morgan tour, not so personal or detailed.

Back on the bikes and could we find a campsite!! Impossible. So 5.00 we went to see Ron and Paul – friends of Ron from Townsville. They said we could stay for the night. So we had beans on toast and chatted to them and watched a bit of their telly. They've a Land Rover, boat, caravan. Ron has a 175 Honda and Paul a 250 Ducatti. Nice blokes. John, a friend of theirs came over after he and Paul had been to a bike meeting. Paul knew Mick from the BMW club in Sydney and had some photos of them all and Mick and his Velo. The three of us slept on the double bed – sheer luxury except Linda kept spraying the mozzies during the night.

(Jacky: I remember sitting outside Ron and Paul's caravan and one of them came home from work. I felt really embarrassed because we were sitting right in his path and he had to ask us to move so he could get in his caravan – really very funny.)

12th May 1972 Mt Isa

13840 341 miles

Had toast and savs (saveloys) for breakfast. Crept out of the caravan to load our bikes at the back by the side way as the caretaker was there! Jacky and Linda did an oil change in the garage. The countryside gradually got worse less rocks and rugged scenery to flat plain horizons. Hundreds of miles in between each petrol stop. Only one pump/store and beer. Pretty isolated. Filled up Camoweal about lunchtime, it was in fact a town, several garages and stores. Had a milkshake – made of powdered milk! Had a can of beer SWAN. 40c each at Barry Caves, just the one station. Several dead cows on the road. Hawks everywhere. A lot of empty drums on the side of the road. Budgies in groups darting about.

I rode the Honda for the next 95 miles to Frewana. The flies are indescribable. Once you stop they settle on you in swarms, hundreds of them crawling and buzzing. We keep our helmets goggles and scarves on as much as possible. A mob of cattle 'cowboys' in here talking about their herd of cattle. Petrol .58c super hamburger .50c. Have just been to the loo. What a laugh – no doors! The shower floor is covered in a muddy pool and a plant climbing through the corrugated fence! The children wear net bags over their heads to keep the flies away. They crawl up your nose, in the corners of your eyes, where they irritate and can start an infection. In the bar after 25c sandwiches we sat writing and reading.

Coach of schoolgirls giggling went through. A load of jackaroos were in the bar and eventually started talking. Fascinating hearing all about their work. 7 days a week approx. 8.00 to 6.00. If the herd is restless and takes time to get back they can be as late as 9.00 in getting back. Only young, done this work since leaving school. Solitary life, couldn't stand the towns. $12.00 clear award rate. Good food, do their own washing. Stayed talking till 1.30 pm drinking.

WE CASH CHEQUES

Picture of back end of a cow

(Jacky - I was talking to the jackeroos and seemed to spend quite some time with one fellow who charmed me with stories of his horse who was called Jacky)

13th May 1972 Frewana

14181 105 miles

All woke up with hangovers. The flies just swarmed although there was a wind and the temp. was lower so they weren't as bad as normal. Left 9.15am still feeling rough. Did the 95 miles to Three Ways, then 15 miles south to Tennant Creek.

Lots of letters. Two bills from the Royal Perth Hospital so I wrote uncollected and sent them back. Got my bank passbook back, thank goodness. Went into a milk bar. Lots of Aborigines here. The town just seems to consist of milk bars! We were reading our mail. Also they have fresh milk here – luxury so we all brought some. Petrol at Frewana 58c gallon.

Don Dobie walked in and said the blokes from the PO had phoned him up and told us we were in town. News travels fast! We went to the campsite 70c each my boy! Had showers and Jacky and I went into town where no branch bank so I could only withdraw $50 from the PO. Had another milk drink and went back – Linda trying to sleep off the delayed reaction of the drink.

Don coming here at 5.00 pm and we're going out for our tea.

Don came round in his Volkswagen beach buggy (red and orange). Chris, the boy from the PO, came and we went to the Boomerang Restaurant. Fantastic. Don bought us our meal. I had Wiener Schnitzel , Jacky hamsteak, Linda porterhouse. Then to the pub. Still with hangovers we managed to drink a few stubbies!

(*Linda: We had met Don Dobie at the Southern Cross Rally in Adelaide. He had given us his address at the PMG in Tennant Creek, where he was working at the time, and said be sure to look him up when we came through*)

14th May 1971 Tennant Creek

14286 390 miles

This morning after being a bit cold during the night I woke up a bit early while the others slept till about 8.30. We went into town posted our letters. I withdrew $50, brought some coffee and left about 10.50. Reached Renner Springs about 12.30 where we had their celebrated sandwiches. You only have one cos you couldn't eat more. They're huge. Home made bread cut really thick and chunks of beef, no skinny wafer bit. Really filling 30c. Ordered 3 more for our tea tonight. Then 97 miles to Newcastle Water which is 2 miles off the Highway and dirt. Here the pace was so slow you have to go into the store to ask them to come out and serve petrol!!. It was one of the old glass pumps. Then we went another 70 odd to Daly Waters where the bloke took a photo of us and he'd just taken one of the coach that had pulled out! Loads of Aboriginal women and picaninnies. The men with beer cans. Friday perhaps they'd just received pay or allowance from welfare?

We'd hoped to make Katherine but decided on Mataranka Homestead. Got quite dark when we reached the turn-off which was 5 miles of dust, gravel and corrugation which we took very slowly. They've a tropical pool which is warm 75 degrees natural. Quite nice, popular. Some Aborigines had just caught a barramundi about 40-60lb. Huge, lying on the pub floor. I can hear laughter from different camp fires. Several safari coaches here. Not the sort of holiday I'd fancy. Normally up about 7.00am, Company provided tents (which the people put up)and mattresses. About three weeks they last. Impossible to see what you want to – just not enough time. Some have cooks.

Loads of anthills as in Queensland but there they were straighter and smaller than here, NT, where they're large and either straight, big and rounded (some fantastic shapes – gorillas with baby on back!)

Saw heap of bleached white bones side of the road. Not so many hawks or eagles (probably cos more trees – not so open) Seen a couple of pure white trunk trees very unusual. Sandwiches were a bit dry in fact none of us felt v. hungry! Odd!

(Jacky: Those sandwiches at Renner Springs – like nothing I have seen since! They were of homemade bread, fresh and thickly cut, piled with meat, beef or lamb, can't remember which. We all had one at lunch time and bought some to have later for dinner but were still so full we couldn't finish them that night!))

Ron Tiemstre on his white BMW

Main road from Townsville to Mt Isa

Another puddle! Main road from
Townsville to Mt Isa

Mt Isa mines

Jacky and Angie at Mt Isa mines

Jackaroos at Frewana

CHAPTER SIXTEEN

——

MATARANKA TO DARWIN

Angie's Diaries:
15th May 1971 Mataranka
14676

Jacky and Linda had a good time talking to the Centralian Coach driver. $150 a week they earn! Went for a swim in the 92 degree hot springs pool. Just like a bath, not as exhilarating as a cold swim. Comes from the ground at 102 degrees and cools on top to 92 degree.

Reached Pine Creek about 1.15 pm and as we pulled into the Station four blokes on BMs rolled up. What an unusual sight! So we all went into the pub for a few beers and were asked to go with them to UDP Falls (*this is now part of Kakadu N.P.)* which was 66 miles of dirt east. Linda wanted to go, Jacky was indifferent and I didn't. We all went in the end. The first 60 miles section was fairly good. Gravelly and badly corrugated more like the Nullarbor but Jacky and Linda kept up. Once we turned off the six miles to the Falls was where the fun began! Mud ridges, sand, deep creeks, you name it, it was there.

Brad rode Linda's BMW through one bad creek which Jacky managed to thrash through. On the way back it was reversed. I think Brad felt good doing his Samaritan act. My handbag fell off the back of Linda's bike. I was on the back of Steven's new 750 BMW. Craig dropped his old BMW on some rocks and badly grazed his arm and knocked the rear carrier off! Further on Mick (the Australian boy, who rode his bike overland) fell off and it was then discovered that further back he must have knocked two holes in the sump on some of the rocks. The water during the tropical rain had been right over the road, only a few weeks back and large sections of the road were awash. The last bit was done with the sun straight in our eyes and dust everywhere reflecting each penetrating particle.

Were we relieved to reach the falls and they were lovely. A sheer drop to a dark tropical pool. With pines and vines skirting it and white sands. After gazing at the falls we put up our tent while the others swam. It was too late for us to swim as it was dark and frankly we were too frightened to go in on our own. Tales of Mt Cross and such leaping to mind. The boys made a fire and we combined our food and had curry and rice. They had brought some beer which soon disappeared. I went to bed about 9.30 pm feeling absolutely exhausted, I'd watched and felt every inch of the journey. My throat was still sore. Steven and the others mended Mick's sump with my Araldite that night.

(Linda- We always carried things to mend our bikes with and Angie had a tube of Araldite in her handbag. It saved the day!)

16th May 1971 UDP Falls

Mick's bike repaired we all packed and were ready to leave. Craig's lackey broke so he tied his gear on with rope. Brad noticed Linda's muffler adrift and they used an extra bolt from the other one to tighten it. All about to leave and Jacky said, "Is my back tyre flat?" "Yes," I said. So, after Steve's burn on puncture kit didn't burn on, Mick, in all his glory, stuck on a patch with glue. This kept us till 12.30 pm!! Once more into the breach. Pulled Jacky out of two mud packs. So difficult with her steering she did absolutely marvellous to get it through. Steven was the better rider although he went too fast on the last stretch and at times we were just sliding out at the corners. He knew this and said he just wanted to get his bike off the punishment.

We reached the pub first. Were all waiting for Craig. He came in very bloody – he'd cut his arms and side and smashed his bike up. Brad took him to the nursing sister and left the bike in the police station. Steven and Brad towed it in as the right handlebar was broken.

We left Pine Creek about 5.00 pm and rode a couple of hours in the dark stopping once for petrol and once to drop off Craig who was very stiff and sore with Brad's fiancée in their car. We all went to Brad's house where he lives with Sue. Most of the homes were put up by the Government consequently they're very alike on metal stilts with asbestos walls, metal venetian type shutters with huge windows, trouble is you can hear every noise outside. We all had welcome showers and a nice steak and rice meal and a beer. Went to bed about 12.00 and couldn't sleep owing to the outrageous noise from the couple opposite.

(*Jacky – I seem to remember Brad's girlfriend wasn't too happy at him turning up with three females!*)

(*Linda – As we were riding in the dark towards Darwin the sky was orange with fire. They were burning off cane, I believe.*)

<u>17</u> May 1971 Darwin

15123

After washing our clothes they needed two washes and after each one the water was black! They had four lovely puppies from their dog and we were tempted to get one to sit on the tank and come with us! Feeling and looking much cleaner we went into town and picked up our letters and looked round the so called city! It's a mere town in size. The only large store being a Woolworths. What a monopoly. As few small shops, nothing madly gay! There isn't the demand here for souvenirs the bulk of the Aboriginals work going to the east tourist regions or down south to the demand there. No cheap goodies here. We're told we could go on the boat to see a native Corroborree (dance) every day.

We went back to Brad's house as it hadn't taken us very long to look round the town. We packed up as our clothes were dry. Mick came in. No tee shirt or ripped jeans but smart trousers and shirt, wasn't working as he is a Wharfie and there was no ship in. But getting appearance money. Cushy number. Bumped into Nancy and Ernie in the GPO (a couple touring in a campervan). Arrived at the camp site about 4.00 had cup of tea with Nancy and Ernie, put up the tent, had a swim in the pool, and tea of peas and pie sitting in the tent. Steven rolled up so he sat in the tent and we had a general run down on the ride and bikes. Discovered that he's married and with a 2 ½ yr old child. Out of the four of them we'd all thought he was the least likely to be married or living with anybody. Thus we had an early night.

18th May 1971 Darwin

Got up 8.30 Nancy and Ernie still packing. Linda's given them Terry's address in WA so perhaps we'll see them again – hope so, they're a terrific couple. So much go! Left eventually after postcard writing 10.30am. Went to Howard Springs 10c to get in, warm water, nothing there, lots of mummies with their kiddies. Into town for a counter lunch 75c steak mushrooms and rice – not as good as Queens Arms (*in Adelaide*) Then we went along by the coast to the defence area and saw the old gun turrets. I guess they used them during the war. Then to the Botanical Gardens. Fairly small. Hoped to see the Aboriginal collection of arts and crafts but it was shut. We were quite hot. It's so humid. Between November and December they have the highest suicide rate for the year. This is the heat and humidity, I can imagine how unbearable it must be. The women don't bother much with make-up as it just pours off!! Quite overcast actually.

When we got back I went mad and cut some of my hair off the top. Come 7.30 pm it wasn't dry and Jacky and Linda had decided to take a few beers over to Brad's place. Steven said he'd be going over too (must have an agreement with his wife!). I'm writing and I've just heard the BMW come back. They were out and they've brought a few stubbies.

19th May 1971 Darwin

Went into town about 9.30am and had a look round the Chinese Temple. It's meant to be a temporary affair as its all corrugated metal. White and a few red wooden trimmings. Inside its fairly elaborate in true Chinese style. Red silk embroidered lengths of material suspended across the hall. Paper and plastic flowers and figures set in displays. Tended to look rather cheap and gaudy.

Then we went to catch the boat for Mica Beach by 10.00am. Took about 1/2hr but when we got to the beach which is at the other end of the harbour we had to wait for about another half hour while they repaired or replaced the battery in 'the Duck' the ex-army landing machines used during the war. Eventually we landed on the beach. Welcomed ashore by the German owner. We had sandwiches .30c and soft drink .25c and then went onto the beach to swim and burn till the Corroboree (dances telling stories) which was at 3.15 pm. Nice beach and lovely sea. He said it was safe to swim they hadn't had any stingers or wasps that year.

There were six men and one woman performing the dances, with the white and yellow paint marked on them which they got from local clay. It was funny the proprietor introduced them each and they said their name, all in good English. In fact the first one, who's a school teacher, even sounded slightly cockney! Happy Dance, Mud Crab Dance – all similar sort of stomping. They were laughing to themselves as they danced, it was really funny real comedians! Took a collection round. They danced for about 1 hour. Then I had a drink before we left and were talking to Robert the school teacher while they had beers. Said farewell and back to the boat.

Mick was on the quayside. Wanted us to go for a swim 6.00!! Went back to the campsite had beans and minced steak and I had rice. Who should bowl up but TONY!(*Tony Harter from Adelaide*), quite unexpected really. I'd been waiting for him to appear. He hadn't liked the trip much up to Alice. Had stayed there a week and then up to Darwin where he was working.

We then started to watch the film 'Hold On' Herman's Hermits which the campsite had put on for .40c. Tony came back after his tea and brought us back the beers we had given him the money for. Then two blokes he'd met at the Overlander on Hondas came back and then Steven, what an understanding with his wife! So they sat on the ground watching. Then we gave them coffee.

20th May 1971 Darwin

Got to Honda's and Jacky's putting a new chain on. Took some time to do it. The mechanic was very nice and did it in his lunch time. But Jacky felt terrible afterwards as he wanted her to go out with him! We left there and went into town. Linda picked up some letters and we had a drink while she read them. On the way back they did an oil change at the Shell Garage. Went for a swim when we got back to the site. An Italian bloke (he had been out 21 years) but could still hear the slight accent. Determined to throw me in and get my hair wet as I was trying to keep it dry. Later that night he succeeded much to Tony's amusement, he'd met them coming over.

Linda:

Although we went to see the gun turrets and took photos of them we didn't actually take in the significance of their presence there.

Darwin was Australia's front line against the Japanese invasion during WW2 and, in fact, during a bombing raid in February 1942, there were more bombs dropped on Darwin than on Pearl Harbour. The city suffered dreadfully and it was in its defence, to transport military equipment, that the road to Darwin from the railhead in Alice Springs (1000miles) was sealed in the 1940's, the southern part to Adelaide not until the late 1970's.

Linda, Nancy, Ernie, Jacky

Bent bike after UPD Falls run

Aboriginal dancers

Darwin's WW2 guns

DARWIN TO ALICE – 1971
(ALICE TO ADELAIDE VIA TRAIN)

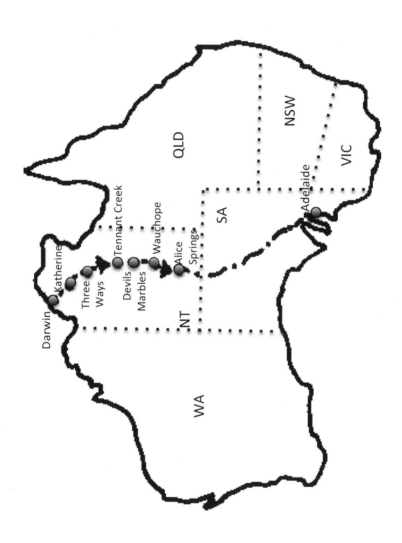

CHAPTER SEVENTEEN

DARWIN TO ALICE

Angie's Diaries:
21ˢᵗ May 1971 Darwin
250mls

As usual we moved out fairly late. Went into each cycle shop (two actually!) Then three garages before we could get some lackeys, (*another name for them is bungey cords or oki straps*). Linda bought two. A very nice road out of Darwin (not bad in either!!) very windy, plenty of dips. Got to Katherine Gorge about 6.30. A dirt road to it. I went in for a swim and we discovered it was $3.00 for the boat trip to see the Gorges. This we thought was a bit steep and taking the tourist for what he could get!! Were on the way there, I rode Jacky's Honda from Pine Creek and when we went down to see the Gorge, Linda following braked on some gravel to pick up a lackey which had just fallen off the Honda. This brought the bike down and Jacky cut her hands and Linda bruised herself!

We bought biscuits for tea with our coffee and then a bloke came up and asked if we were going to Darwin and to join the BMW Club. Linda said "Why? Who do you know in Darwin with a BMW?" He was from Darwin – Greg, and knew Steve, Craig, Brad. Invited us over for female company to his campsite. Another bloke Mick, photographer, and he was a journalist. Just after what they could get. The boat guide (from London) came up (cosy threesome) knew hardly anything about the Gorges and used to pipe a lot of yarns.

Manager of the site gave a party for his wife's birthday! So we all had a dance! Back to their fire and after getting rid of Greg went to bed . No free boat trip for any of us!!!!

22ⁿᵈ May, 1971
15543 306 mls

Left the Gorge about 9.45am and onto the dirt to Katherine which took us about ½ hr. Jacky filled up and we went to the Katherine Caves about 25 miles out of Katharine. Jacky and I not being cave fans sat it out and read the guide's wife's magazines. Linda said the caves were quite good, there were coloured lights. Also the evidence of the stay of a man who'd stayed in the caves for 63 days in 1962, he didn't need any water it seemed as he was well equipped with Swan! Then we stopped at Mataranka had a beer and pie in the garden, it was quite nice. Linda put on all our favourite records.

(Linda- The favourite at the time was 'I never promised you a Rose Garden'. As there was one tatty looking rose in the garden at the roadhouse I thought it was appropriate and ever afterwards I think of that pub stop when I hear the song.)

Jacky adjusted her chain, stretched already, probably the sprocket is that badly worn now! Then we stopped at Daly Water, Jacky and Linda refuelled .56c here. Atrocious! Saw two wild emus run across the road and two absolutely huge eagles swoop off as we came nearer. Lovely yellow flowered trees on either side.

Stopped at Elliot for the night next to the public toilets. Played cards in the Mobil Café till 9.30 pm. All quite tired. Vast quantities of rubber from the blown tyres on the sides of the road, tubes and complete tyres. Such waste – beer bottles, pop cans littered everywhere. People write their names on prominent rocks alongside the highway – stupid.!

23 May 1971 Elliot

15849

We left 10.00am, flies were getting worse as the morning wore on. Stopped at Renner Springs for a huge beef sandwich – those famous ones again. Then another 100 miles to Tennant Creek. Found Don, Chris and Barry Lang at the hostel. Typical Sunday afternoon. Arrived about 3.00. Chris was washing. Barry had taken his gear box out. Don was just looking for an excuse to just sit and drink his beer which we were armed with. Went in the hostel where they said we could stay. Geoff White from the Bank was there washing his car. They cooked us tea. It was gorgeous, chips, sausage and egg and toast, so well cooked, talk about domesticated. Jacky and Linda had one spare room and I had another. Sheer bliss beds!!! They persuaded us into staying on Monday so we could go to the Bank BBQ. Had an early night – felt we needed it after the day and the beers helped.

24th May, 1971 Tennant Creek

Went into town by 9.00 so we weren't at the PMG Hostel when the cleaning woman came. Got all our mail – piles plus Geoff's- and brandy!!! Took photo of the famous miles signpost. Then we went out to Peko Mine. Eyes staring at us from everywhere as well as whistles. Went into the General Office and the receptionist (whom we met at the BBQ that night – everybody knows everybody!) gave us helmets and told us where not to go. Therefore there was hardly anything to see. Flies were terrible.

Back to Tennant and got our lunch - curry and rice! The cleaning woman had gone. 12.00. Don and Barry came for lunch. The cleaning woman had seen Don and said, "Did you have someone staying?" "Yes a bloke and then two girls". "What Department?" " PMG Adelaide!!" Had our lunch when they'd gone.

I did Jacky's and my washing. Linda did hers Sunday. Wrote letters, then went into town to buy carton stubbies. Had started drinking them by the time they got home. All felt merry. Put on dresses, we all felt quite ladylike. Off in the beach buggy. We spent most of the time talking to Don, Barry, Geoff and new boy to bank, Gary. Barry was the only one who danced with Linda and I. Steak, sausage and bread – lovely. But alas too much beer! Left about 1.00 and Barry and Don showed us where they worked. Extremely technical. Then back for coffee and thankfully bed.

25th May, 1971 Tennant Creek

16038 313 mls

Didn't feel too bright. We were up at 8.00 and packed and left by 8.45 to avoid the cleaning woman. A bit of road repairs out of the Creek. First stop Wauchope, filled up. Next stop Barrows Creek where we had a pie. It was getting pretty cold. Stopped to look at the Devil's Marbles before Wauchope. Fantastic ! Quite a phenomena. So many of these smooth rounded rocks which look as if they've fallen from the sky. Ghastly little people have written their names over some.

Got into Alice Springs about 3.00pm. Like the first impression. We went to Viv and Deanna Johnson's motor cycle shop on Leichart Street – she said "'we've been expecting you" as Don had phoned them up on Sunday. Spoke to Deanna for a while. She said the caravan was empty that Don had lived in so we paid the $10.00 for a week. Very good. Much better than a tent (plates –china cups, stove, blankets, mattress) this is living!

Went into town. It's very modern and clean lots of Aborigines about. Got our mail. Tried to look up Spud Murphy, friend of Don's.

Told to come back so after our egg sandwich tea we called back at 7.30pm. Lives in a house with several others. Got a new BMW, sings at the folk club. Long blonde hair. Friend Dave, his girlfriend Libby, live there. All like Alice. Had several cups of coffee and left about 9.30. Glad to leave.

26 May 1971 Alice Springs

Got up 9.30am!! It was so cold last night. Even in sleeping bag and with blankets. Left about 11.00 and went to Stanley Chasm in order to be there by 12 noon as that's when the sun shines directly into the chasm. Twenty five miles out then a turn off of 6 1/2 miles of dirt to it. Quite rough and so we were going pretty slow. Coachload of American tourists there also. It was lovely, such red rock.

Came back to the kiosk and bought some artefacts. Made at the native reserve near Alice Springs. Jacky & Linda bought a shield-type wooden thing. Linda and I bought carved animals. Had a drink and then up the road to Simpson's Gap and again dirt road. This is a gap in the rock ranges and there was a water pool in between. Got some rocks from there. Mauve, white, tan and pink coloured. Beautiful.

Stopped at Flynn's Memorial, where his ashes are. Back into town to the PO and looked round the shops at all the souvenirs and there's enough of them really tempting. Spoke to a girl who'd hired a 120 Suzuki from Johnsons. Been where we had that day $3.00 per day and 5c per mile – from Perth. Back to the van and curry and rice. Spud popped in we're going round there tomorrow night. Washed my hair and generally did bugger all.

27th May 1971 Alice Springs

Got up at 9.00. We left for the Pitchie Ritchie Museum abut 9.45 and arrived there 10.00 as it's only a few miles out of town. 20c entrance. A lot of clay sculptures by William Ricketts were displayed in the grounds. Nicely done, set amongst rocks. A tribute to the Aboriginal painter Albert Namatjira was set up. It's a bird sanctuary as well, but I only saw two birds. A lot of old mining and well drilling equipment. Surprised they hadn't appeared to have restored (no not restored – just preserved it to prevent further rotting) for a lot of the drays and wagons were surely going that way.

Got back to town and started our enquiries into the Ayers Rock trip. Had pies and then Jacky and Linda went to the Commonwealth

Employment while I went to the GPO and bought a cravat for Geoff. Nothing at the Bureau. Then booked for our safari trip with Sampson Tours – 2 day $27.00 to Ayers Rock and The Olgas. Bought our food rations for the trip.

Then to the Flying Doctor Base. Very interesting – bought a key ring. First flight in 1928 - the first base was Cloncurry. A sister would go to accompany the patient on the way back. Each outpost has a medical chest with an assortment of medical needs. Symptoms would be heard by the base from a homestead by radio and then diagnosis and action given. If thought necessary patient would be brought in. Partly Government subsidised, the rest donations. Then to GPO and out to the Old Telegraph Station and National Park. Very pretty there. Also the original springs. A small spring which during the wet becomes flooded to quite a distance. Used to use a pedal –operated machine to generate electricity which was used to power the Morse code which was typed on a transmitter to the base. They then brought in speaking over the line intercom system.

The town was originally called Stuart after the first explorer in the area. Renamed Alice Springs after Charles Todd's Superintendent of Telegraphs, wife, Alice. Confusion arose between the railway station called Stuart and the Springs called Alice (where the old telegraph station stands) so it became Alice Springs. Back to our van and egg sarnies. Going to Spud Murphy's for a few beers. Terrible boring evening. He buggered off when we arrived for 2 hrs!

28th May 1971 Alice Springs

On returning last night was this boy who was talking to Viv. He has got a Honda 4, red tank, 1969. Has done 36,000 miles on it. Replaced 4 chains (every 10,000 he does that.) Had just arrived from Adelaide on the South Road, the last 120 miles he'd done in the dark. The only bloke (apart from Don Dobie) who hadn't fallen off on the dirt!! Was off to Wyndham to work. He had coffee with us and we went to bed quite late.

This morning we went to the Anzac Hill, the view over Alice. Boy was it cold! Then over the river (which is nearly always dry-apart from in the Wet) Here we went to Battarbee Art Gallery. Rex Battarbee has his paintings on display, also Albert Namatjira, who Battarbee tutored. Another room of his son's and grandson's work and other Aboriginal artists. A lot of paintings and reproductions, bark paintings, books, Aboriginal arts all for sale! I bought a bark painting $9.00.

We went into town to the Flynn Memorial Church and museum at the back with information on John Flynn's work. I bought our rations for the two day trip to the Rock, Ryvita and luncheon beef and sardines. Jacky and Linda had Bush Biscuits (taste like morning coffee) and cheese. Drew out some more money.

Went to the railway station and they found out how much their bikes would cost them. Jacky's thinking of leaving her bike on till Adelaide owing to the bad condition of the chain and sprocket.

(Linda – The South Road from Alice Springs was in terrible condition at that time as it was not yet paved. As it was almost 1000miles we felt it was beyond our capabilities and were therefore going to put the bikes on The Ghan train for the trip south).

Then back to the van where Charlie was busy working on his bike. Cleaned the fork seals and drained the oil, general service. Then did Jacky's bike for her. Adjusted the tappets which were very tight and much longer left they would have holed the piston. Cleaned the oil filter – which was full of muck, did the points and it sounds tremendous! Tender loving care. Did our washing. Went to the GPO, wrote loads of letters telling everyone the wedding date.

Viv invited us for beer and we went inside. They have two children. Then Charlie and us three had tea – fish and few chips, peas, beans, mixed together with camp pie and rice! Huge. Then some of Charlie's fruit. He went about 8.30 and we went to bed about 11.00 none of us slept till 2.00am.

CHAPTER EIGHTEEN

———

AYERS ROCK AND ANGIE'S DEPARTURE

Linda:
The road out to the famous Australian icon Ayers Rock, now called by its Aboriginal name, Uluru, was 300miles each way of really bad dirt, sand, bulldust and corrugations. We knew that it was not for us to do on bikes and therefore had decided to go by tourist bus. It was possible to camp almost next to the Rock in those days and prices weren't as high as they are today. We made a booking and prepared for the trip.

Angie's Diaries:
29th May 1971 Alice Springs
    Linda dropped Charlie's wireless but luckily it was nothing serious and he mended it. Waited till 9.45am for the coach meant to have left at 9.00. I gave them a ring. Posted the letters this morning and nearly froze on the way. We were expecting a large express coach – chilled water, toilet, air conditioning, reclining chairs. No such luck – it's an over- sized combie van bus. We're travelling overnight and there are just upright seats. Dust literally wafting through the air. No toilet, no water. Couldn't stand upright.
    There were eleven passengers and the driver. The two old ladies in front were really cut up about the trip and are hoping to fly back! The road is really bad and once you turn off the South Road to Ayers Rock it's all thick dust. Linda was quite happy as she sat at the very front next to the driver. No sickness. Jacky and I sat at the very back with plenty of room.
    The coach was going everywhere so was the dust. Bumping, sliding, going from lock to lock. Some real bad sand drifts! Apart from the ride we arrived at the Rock 5.30 pm and our driver Norm took us to see the sunset over Ayers. I took a photo at 6.00pm and one after the sun had gone to see the difference. Back and put our tent up acquired two mattresses from the cabin!! More comfortable.

Going to the pub – would you believe! Found out the beer was 45c a stubby – the most expensive we've ever found in Australia. So after one beer we all went to bed. Had a marvellous night's sleep.

30th May, 1971 Ayers Rock

Woke up at 8.00am and having packed everything to wear we were warm that night despite what everyone had thought. It had been 32F degrees one night! Had a coffee. Left at 9.00am went round to the Climb of Ayers Rock. The Rock is 1180ft high and we climbed to the very top. Left at 9.20 and after stopping at frequent intervals, there's a safety rail to help you up the steep bits. The first is fairly steep the second section is very undulating and quite sheer drops in parts. A girl ran past me, she works at the Rock and does it every morning. Today in 19 mins. I did it in about 43 mins. Linda next in socks! 45 mins and the rest followed between 5 to 10 mins later. It was quicker on the way down although quite a strain on the legs. There's a book on top for signatures. Got down in 25 mins and had a very welcome drink. It was quite windy higher up.

We left there and went to the airstrip. Here, everyone but us and one of the women's husbands went up. $3.00 to see the aerial view of the Rock and $6 to see the Olgas as well. Took a photo of the Brain as marking on one face of the Rock. Also a photo of the Kangaroo Tail. A rock form in a long strip with a gap in one section through which you could see light. Then round the caves. One side the men's caves and the other the women's caves.

Seems the Aboriginals came there from their own tribal area for ceremonies. For this they were allowed to pass through other tribal areas as long as they didn't stop. They came to the Rock as here was water. After the caves we went back to the motel where I had coffee with my sardines and Ryvita. Then, as the brakes had failed on our coach, Norm, our coach driver, got us another ride on a Pioneer Express, with some others. We went out to the Olgas to the Gorge. They're 20 miles from Ayers Rock. A different structure to the Ayers. Ayers being sandstone, Olgas is made up of compressed rock(conglomerate), rounded boulders. One I acquired. Lovely colouring and joined together, cemented into large mounds. Then, after we'd collected some wood, we moved off to a fireplace and had billy tea! And biscuits! Lucky us!

Then at about 4.00 we went to the Valley of the Winds, where there was no wind! But very interesting. Here I got my rock. Lovely blue fleck inside. We saw a leseto (?) which looks like a wallaby but has long hair. Then as we carried on back we saw absolutely loads of kangaroos, another photo. By this time it was after five hence the animal life. Then suddenly Mal, the driver shouted "Look, a dingo!" He ran straight across the track in front of us with something in his mouth. Didn't run away but stopped at the side of the road and once we had passed turned and back to the track to picking what he'd dropped on being startled.

Waited to watch the sunset on the Rock but it wasn't any good. Too much cloud. Back to the motel and I had a coffee! Then Norm said a friend of his, owner of another motel was going to show some of his slides and we could see them too. They were very good. Unbelievable the different colours the rock will show. When there has been rain which they had after a drought of 9 years in 1966? The flowers after two weeks of rain just filled the ground for hundreds and hundreds of miles as far as the Simpson Desert. Ground which was once totally bare! Beautiful photos of the Olgas and sunsets and sunrises such unique colouring to Australia.

Two bags of crisps later we went back to the Motel. I wrote a postcard to Geoff to get the Ayers Rock postmark. We departed in our luxury little van. Everyone in good spirits. The two older ladies having decided to fly back and have a nasty word with Sampsons Tours. Stopped at Curtain Falls and that was it. Norm kept up a good speed.

31st May 1971 Ebenezer/Alice Springs

What a night; a few hours dozing in between rude awakenings at the jolts in the road. We stopped for about half an hour and managed to just fall asleep and wake up, I couldn't, being unaccustomed to the sudden silence. We had a blanket each. The sleeping bags as pillows but no one was able to stretch full out. My eyes just kept dropping, no position was comfortable for long. I don't remember passing any other vehicles either way. - Are we the only fools?! After 1.30 am I remembered checking my watch every few hours dozing fitfully in between. Everyone was quiet except for Ernie's wife who occasionally muttered about something to him. I knew we must be getting near at 5.30am and expected the sunrise but alas it never came. Staying awake nearly all night becomes quite acceptable if you're able to watch the beauty of a sunrise. Seems it's not till quite later 7-7.30am.

Ernie and his wife got off first at the C/P Pitchie Ritchie. Then we got off, which left two boys and a young couple, Valerie and Barry. Jacky and I went to bed after a cup of coffee. I felt a bit sick. Linda wrote letters. She woke us up at 8.30 after two hours sleep with a cup of coffee. We both felt better for it. My legs ache at the knees after all yesterday's climbing.

Went into town. No jobs for Jacky and Linda. I drew out $40. Brought my Pioneer coach ticket to Adelaide, Wednesday, $29.00. Bought some curry! Did a bit of packing and did some washing. Read a bit. Had our curry. Read some more. Linda went to bed at 7.00. Jacky and I started reading. About 7.00 Viv came to the door. He had a letter from Don Dobie saying he was coming down for the weekend. I wrote to say I wouldn't be here. Went to bed about 9.00 Jacky and I having finished off the bread and beans. Long time to get to sleep.

(Linda – Angie was going back to Adelaide on the Pioneer bus. She was going to arrange her wedding , to book the Registry office for herself and Geoff's ceremony and for Terry and me the following weekend.)

1st June 1971 Alice Springs

Its pouring with RAIN! Didn't wake up till late and got up even later. No coffee left. We made off for town. Jacky and Linda went to the Commonwealth, they go first for a chat with Bob Fraser, friend of Doris, for there's never any work! I bought the bread and marg for our tea, plus some fruit for the coach journey. Went back to the van. Still raining. Felt strange to be wearing PVC's and scarves. Heads down all huddled. Had coffee and some bread.

Left about 12.30 and we went to the library. We were there till 4.00. Reading magazines. Went to the PO. Linda had a letter from Ron Tiemstre. Will visit here 9th June as he's coming over to Mt. Isa. Walked slowly back. Still raining. Had ice cream on the way. Read and wrote letters. A general thing is letter writing when you've got nothing to do. Had our sausage sandwiches. I washed my hair, absolutely filthy after the dust from Ayers Rock trip. My packing's practically done. Playing cards. Linda's going to get some dry ginger for the brandy Geoff sent me. These two months have sure gone quickly. We all had two glasses each and played cards till ll.00pm.

2nd June 1971 Alice Springs

I got up at 7.30 am, made the coffee and then finished my packing. Boy, are the saddlebags heavy! I've taken as many souvenirs of Jacky and Linda as I could pack. Said goodbye to Deanna and Viv. Commonwealth phoned – Jacky was going to try for the job. Viv gave us a lift to the coach depot. No coach so after Viv went we went off for a coffee and toast till 9.30 am. Still no coach till we got closer and saw it had been parked in a lane for sometime!

Threw my sand and dust riddled saddle bags to be loaded. Jacky had returned from Employment Bureau. No answer yet. Had to get on coach, then off again, suddenly I remembered my bark painting. Quick as a flash Jacky shot back and came running back with it just in time (it was a long way back) the coach driver was a very jovial bloke, young from Yorkshire. I had a marvellous seat, at the very front at the aisle - wide view right in front! Only 10 of us and he kept saying not enough to push us out of a bog.

Dot was the woman who sat to my right. Soon barriers were broken. It was Dot's sixth trip! The three of us chatting away. Nobody else on the coach seemed to say anything. Very overcast and gradually in the afternoon we came into rain. Stopped about 3.00 for a pie. Next couple of hours went quickly, Brian, the driver, and I discussing England etc.!! 7.30 they changed drivers and Norman got in. Read for quite a bit then realised everyone's lights were out so 10.45 I turned mine off. We hit some roos, "just touched that's all" as he saw them and slowed down.

The road was gradually getting worse, we were ahead of time. They're only allowed to do 40 mph on the dirt; not because it's easier it sure aint! But 'cos they've had so many suspensions and axles messed up through hitting pot holes at high speed that the Company forbid it. On the bitumen anything goes. Also their speeding fines go to the driver! Sat watching the road and eyes shutting, very hard to keep your eyes open in the dark without a cause.

11.30 pm we pulled up at Coober Pedy. Mighty miner land. Into the pub which was still going only sandwiches available though no one had had a hot meal all day. Didn't worry me but did the people used to good food!! Sandwiches 25c. I had coffee and eventually had a beer 20c for 6 ozs. I didn't even feel it, could have been water. 95% men. Bar shut a little later and just before we were leaving was asked to dance! Declined politely and ten minutes later we left.

3rd June 1971 Port Augusta

Back on the coach and everybody seemed to be reading so I read for a bit. Had arranged the chair to recline as far as possible which isn't much and all my gear stacked up on the floor to try and make it level with the seat so I could put my feet out level. It didn't work and every hour I kept waking up trying to find a more comfortable position. Your back's always bent or your legs curled up. Couldn't do it for many nights! Nice and warm however in my sleeping bag.

Heard the new driver get on 5.00am and 6am the sun was coming up a brilliant beautiful yellow, nearly made it worth waking up for!! Dot had a good night's sleep. That's because she's so small and tiny, she just curled up on the seat. Sat watching the road, a nice clear day.

The road in patches was terrible the mud was terrible, deep and ridged. Not very good for the bikes! Reached Port Augusta by about 12.30 pm and into the garage café. There Dot and I had a hamburger, the bloke behind Dot on the coach had a mixed grill – it looked delicious.

The bitumen seemed quite boring after the dirt, it's amazing how you take it for granted. Coming into Adelaide the traffic getting heavy, the numbers of people increasing. I turned and looked at Dot and her fellow companion - his eyes were wide and I said "overwhelming isn't it?! He said "No - frightening." He was right.

Linda at Three Ways

Johnsons Motorcycle shop at Alice Springs

Northern Territory sign

Our bus to the rock

Ayers Rock

CHAPTER NINETEEN

SOJOURN IN THE ALICE

<u>Linda:</u>

After Angie left on the bus to Adelaide, Jacky and I returned to the caravan feeling a bit bereft. We'd lost our team member. However, we had decided to stay for a month and find work. As it was the winter months, i.e. Alice's tourist season, we had no problem. I became an expert at frying fish and chips, getting the batter 'just right' and learning not to burn the chips. I was a bit perturbed to find that 'flake' was actually shark! We never had that in England- cod country.

It was fun in Alice, especially staying with Viv and Deanna. Their motorcycle business was more like a family affair as they helped all the bike travellers and competition guys and were so open, welcoming to all. Indeed their actual premises *were* open, the showroom being their front lawn displaying the variety of bikes for sale. The back lawn, on which our caravan and another rested, was often camping area for visiting bikers from Tennant Creek, Mt Isa and Darwin.

Once, on a rare day off for them, Viv and Deanna took Jacky and me out bush in their Landrover and opened a huge basket which held all their bush equipment. They called it 'The Tucker Box'. There was a jar of strawberry jam which was for putting on the damper we made in an open fire. When I unscrewed it, it had a skin of mildew on top, being permanently stored in the Landy.

I pointed this out to Deanna and she said nonchalantly, "Oh yes, just scrape it to one side, it won't hurt, after all penicillin was discovered from mould".

I accepted this and whenever my jams or fruit preserves show the same covering I always think of Deanna's advice and just spoon it to one side.

Alice was still very much a bush town in 1971, in splendid isolation and there were a great deal of Aboriginals living there with no outward signs of the social problems of today.

From its initiation in 1872, as a repeater station for the Overland Telegraph, it only became a town proper in 1887 after gold was discovered in Arltunga, about 100kms east, but there was still only a small population. It was WW2 which brought the Alice to prominence and world fame as, with the Japanese attacks on Darwin, and the subsequent civilian evacuation of that town, it became the provisional capital and thousands of troops were stationed in Alice in readiness for their deployment to the front lines in Darwin or New Guinea.

When we arrived it was a happy, lively place. In 1970 the Americans had set up a satellite tracking station at Pine Gap, locally called the Space Base, and so there were several families based there which boosted the economy and ensured that there was plenty of entertainment. Three pubs held a roaring trade. The Riverside (Mona's) The Stuart Arms (on its third rebuild after fires) and the Alice Springs Hotel (Uncles). The Pioneer Theatre provided two different programs a week and there was a drive- in on the airport road. TV was not yet ensconced so shows and theatre were popular and community and sports groups thrived. There were two restaurants as well as counter meals at the pubs and various snack bars, the fish and chip shop where I worked being one of them.

Unfortunately we were going to miss one of Alice's great, world famous annual events that is still going strong and held in September (then in August), the Henley on Todd boat race. Originally a 'piss take' of the Pom's famous boat race it has become an institution. Run in the dry river Todd it uses bottomless boats in which the crews legs are used to propel them.

Being two young, single girls we had plenty of invites to social events, especially as everyone knew the Johnsons and so we were included in theirs. We therefore enjoyed our stay and it was a wrench to leave and catch the train back to Adelaide. Neither of us had the stamina or expertise to conquer the dirt track- a thousand miles of it- down south so we were travelling on the Ghan to Adelaide, the train named after the Afghan camel handlers who came out with the camels used for early inland exploration.

Departing at 8pm we put our bikes in the baggage car and took our seats in the general carriage where we soon found a bunch of guys to drink with. As the journey took two days and nights (if it didn't become derailed) we had a compartment with bunks to sleep in and were even woken by a steward each morning with a cup of tea! The restaurant car provided us with silver service meals too. So our journey was most enjoyable and we were able to view the fascinating, arid desert landscape from the safety of a railway seat, rather than battling through it on corrugations and being covered with bull-dust.

The narrow gauge line ended at Marree so here, at the unearthly hour of 5.15am we had to change trains to continue to Port Pirie arriving about 5pm later that day. Here we unloaded our bikes, donned our helmets once more and, in the chill morning air, rode the rest of the way to Adelaide where we found Angie and Geoff and had many a beer to celebrate our re-union.

Jacky:

I got a job in Alice cleaning in a motel where there seemed to be quite a few long term residents. I used to have a little cleaning trolley that I would push around. Unfortunately, after a couple of weeks I started to have difficulty swallowing. I went to see a doctor at the Alice Springs Hospital who told me I had quinsy and that I needed to be admitted. The hospital was a low, long building in those days and I recall the ward seemed to go on forever with the Aboriginals one end and the rest of us down the other end. Apparently the Aboriginal women would often take off on "walkabout".

I wasn't very prepared for hospital life and didn't have a nightdress to my name. I was given a full length floral winceyette nightdress to wear, for which I was so grateful I 'forgot' to give it back and had many, many years of warmth out of it.

Linda came to visit me in hospital and I told her that one of the nurses was someone we had previously met. She commented that she wouldn't like someone she knew giving her injections in the bum. I didn't care! When I came out of hospital it was time for us to travel back down to Adelaide.

My overriding memory of the journey on the Ghan was what we called "drunken alley". Instead of a straight corridor running the length of the train the corridor wove its way round the sleeping compartments which seemed to be placed on alternate opposite sides. I assume the name came from the amount of drinking we did on the train – wonderful views of the bush and good company made it a remarkable journey.

CHAPTER TWENTY

THE WEDDINGS AND GOODBYE

<u>Angie:</u>
Geoff and I went to the Registry Office and booked our wedding, making sure that we booked Linda's a week later in order that our friends only had to make one long- distance trip. Geoff was at work and so Ginge (Dennis Hodges) who was staying with us, came with me to buy my wedding ring. Arthur Passel's parents had very kindly volunteered to host our reception. In effect they did far more than this – my own contribution being minimal. I 'found' a cake (in the shape of a book) in a local baker's.

My 'hen night' (as they are now called) consisted of us three girls going drinking, getting chatted up and being given a lift to another pub where we came upon Geoff's stag party all looking pretty miserable.

On the day Linda did my hair for me, I put on my best (and only) two piece and off we went. Pete Westerman was the best man and Jacky was witness. The service started with the Registrar, after formally identifying us, asking for the $7.50 fee! He then added "And it will cost you more than that to get out of it"! Rick Bevis passed his hat around...this was to cause a lot of jokes and comments for some time to come.

Lenny Martino was taking us to Mr and Mrs Passel's in his GTO Falcon V8 and we left the Registry Office with spinning wheels and squealing tyres. No horse drawn carriage for us! We stopped at a pub to calm the nerves, and onto our reception. Plenty of food music and booze – Mr and Mrs Passel did us proud!

Arriving back at our flat, a little the worse for wear, I managed to drop the remains of the cake as Geoff was carrying me over the threshold.! Everybody received crumbs!

There was sufficient booze for several parties throughout the week as we waited for Linda's wedding.

Linda:

My hen night was more or less the same as Angie's and all the same people came to both weddings, apart from Terry who had not yet arrived for his work prevented his presence at the first wedding. He came over from Perth by bus and Paddy (our best man), Joe and Mick, had done the same only a week earlier. After his stag do, Terry stayed the night at the home of Les Duffield, the oldest motorcyclist we knew who, in his late 60s, was still a keen rider on his BMW outfit with his little dog in the sidecar.

My wedding ceremony was also at the Registry office, and we must have had the same celebrant as Angie and Geoff because he made the same joke about it being a damn sight more expensive to get divorced than married. Then the reception was at the home of Jack and Joan Clarke. They were a middle-aged couple from the North of England who had emigrated some years previously and set up home in Adelaide. Jack was a television repair man. Somehow I had become good friends with them, even though they were normal, i.e. didn't ride bikes or play folk music, and they were very kind to all three of us and often invited us around for a meal or just a chat. They were quite happy to host my wedding and we all helped prepare the buffet food the day before. Apparently Joan sent me out to get some sweet corn for the salad and I came back with a can of the creamed variety; she was not impressed. It didn't bode well for my future life of domesticity!

Being winter, the end of June we had to be quite well covered but, as it was the days of the miniskirt, I had made a short, cream dress and wore it with long, brown boots and gloves. I had my false hairpiece arranged on my head too!

After the short ceremony, which was attended by our friends including Bob and Helen Jolly, Pete Westerman, Arthur Passals, Lenny Martino, Rick Bevis, Shirley and Rob Rowe ,Chris Witcombe, Les Duffield and others, we then sojourned to the house to get into some singing, ably led by Paddy and Joe, and a large quantity of beer. When it was time to cut the wedding cake, which Joan had kindly made, I was so tipsy that I nearly cut off Terry's finger.

After the party was over Terry and I rode, in a rather wobbly fashion, to a hotel in Tea Tree Gully and the others likewise drove or rode back to their accommodation in other parts of Adelaide.

Angie and Geoff stayed in Adelaide and later shipped their bike back to UK and took a plane home. Terry and I rode my bike back to Perth where he continued his printing business. Jacky went bush to have a short spell as a housemaid/pump attendant/cook/waitress in the isolated railway town of Kingoonya before taking a flight to New Zealand to continue her travels. She also returned later to UK.

Thus ended our two year adventure together as Three Wandering Poms in the vast land of Australia. It is an experience that the three of us shall never forget.

Jacky, Geoff and Angie

Joan, Jacky and Jack

Angie and Geoff
going to tie the knot

Artie, Paddy, Jacky and Joe

Shirley and Rob Rowe, Helen and Bob
Jolley, Chris Witcombe

The vows

The Wedding Party

Linda and Terry outside
registry office

Jacky, Linda, Terry and Pat at the ceremony

149

POSTSCRIPT

Linda:

Looking back on these experiences from a distance of forty years there are several things that astonish and delight me.

The first is how lucky I was to meet Angie and Jacky at the very beginning of our Australian adventure and how soon we became friends and got on so well together.

Motorcycling was completely new to them and yet they followed my example without question. It was harder for Jacky, obviously very frightening for her, yet she didn't flinch at the experience. I salute her bravery and persistence.

In those days we all had old bikes that were unreliable and it was considered the norm to be able to fix them on the road. Motorcyclists were familiar with the mechanics of their vehicles and would expect to spend time on journeys at the side of the road not only fixing their own bikes but helping others. I had previous experience of this riding in Europe and UK but it was new to Jacky and Angie and Angie, especially, soon acquired an understanding of basic mechanics.

We were three young, attractive girls on the road in a strange country yet we had no fear of the unknown, no thought of ever being molested or mistreated on our journeys. We had no health, travel or breakdown insurance and did not even consider it. We believed in people being there to help us on the road and we would do likewise. On our travels we met many diverse people and appreciated every new experience.

When I first became aware of Angie's diaries in 2005 and she read them out, I was amazed at how accepting she had been of all that I, as the experienced motorcyclist, had led them into. I fully expected to hear some 'whinges' about my probably bossy behavior, but, as you will have read, I seem not to have been too objectionable – or else she has edited them!

I have made many more long journeys by motorcycle around the world and can honestly say that these two girls were the best travelling companions that I ever had and it is with pride that I still count them as my very valuable friends.

All the motorcyclists we met in Australia in those days were great people who showed us friendship and hospitality. They were innovative and independent. It was before the days of 'executive bikers'. Motorcycles were still the poor man's option or the choice of enthusiasts. Most owners did their own servicing on second hand bikes and enjoyed it. Forty years later the motorcycling scene is different but there is still a feeling of camaraderie which will survive.

It has been a long journey down memory lane to put this book together, with Angie's diaries, Jacky's memories and the recollections of other people who met us in those days. I hope that this book has brought back memories for other immigrants from those days and maybe will inspire others to go out and explore without fear or preconceived notions of the unknown.

Linda – 2013

THREE WANDERING POMS

They came from damp old England
A new land for to see
With never much intention
Of staying permanently
It was just for an adventure
A two year term away
Then home to good old Blighty
Perhaps no more to stray

But the new land held surprises
Held a certain latent charm
It taught them undiscovered skills
That they used without a qualm
While gaining self sufficiency
In the new roles they took on
They learnt to give just as they got
Those three wandering Poms

They started off in Sydney
It's there they learnt to ride
Kings Cross showed a few strange sights
But they found the countryside
They conquered the Snowy Mountains
Rode up Capitol Hill
To Melbourne and to Adelaide
Their bikes were running still

The dusty, potholed Nullarbor
Was first of many trials
But they took it in their stride
And ate up all the miles
Whatever hardship came their way
They smiled and battled on
It took more than a bit of dirt to faze
Those three wandering Poms

Then back again to turn up north
And see the many sights
The East coast had to offer
To fill their days and nights
Found coral reefs and waterfalls
Caves and thermal springs
Jackaroos in Queensland
And learnt of cattle kings

Gun battlements in Darwin
The sights of Kakadu
The Devils Marbles by the road
As they passed gaily through
Ayers Rock loomed impressive
And the Olgas purple haze
Then they found work in Alice Springs
To spend the last few days

The Ghan chugged slowly southward
Covered miles to reflect upon
That the shared time was now at an end
For these brave three wandering Poms

NAMES OF PEOPLE IN "THREE WANDERING POMS" IN APPROXIMATE ORDER OF APPEARANCE.

Linda Bootherstone
Jacky Griffin
Angela Griffin (later Branston)
Trevor Green
Harry Fillmore
Jan Buckley (later Thomas)
'Tante' Mrs Lesley Saggers
Anne Bootherstone (later Dungey)
Janet Bootherstone
Philip Bootherstone
Kathy Danvers (nee Griffin)
Veronica Dimmock (nee Griffin)
Jim and Maurie Beresford
Mr and Mrs Beresford
Mick Sturgess
Carol and Charlie Duffil
Peter Westerman
Bob Jolly
Geoff Branston
Helen Bidstrup (later Jolly)
Sandra Davis (later Young)
Dierdre Hatton
Peggy Hyde
Tony Harter
Greg Meikle
Peter Roe
Mrs Meikle
Dennis Hodges (Ginge)
Mr and Mrs Pen
George Sheriff
Beryl and Ken ?
Barbara and Gary?
Andy Scott
John Edwards
Brian Anderson

Richard Evans
Chris Witcombe
Charlie Scott
Terry Bick
Mr and Mrs Bick
Greg Hastings
Eric Nicols
Peter Senior
Brian Cartwright
Trevor and Jenny Luck
Ron MackIntyre, jnr and snr.
Don Chesson
Peter Fougere
Maurice Farmer
Paddy McLoughlan
Joe and Mick ?
Trevor Thomsett
Stan Ogden
Barry Ryan
Peter Mitchell
Dave Bush
Brian Sprawson
John Galvin
Geoff Howie
Peter Gleeson
Penny Lawson
Ron Tiemstre
Don Dobie
Brad, Steven , Craig and Mick ? (boys from Darwin)
Nancy and Ernie?
Viv and Deanna Johnson
Spud Murphy
Charlie? (Viv and Deanna's mechanic)
Lenny Martino
Les Duffield
Bob and Shirley Rowe
Jack and Joan Clarke
Arthur Passalls
Mr and Mrs Passals

Rick Bevis

The authors would be grateful if anyone mentioned in this book would like to give feedback or just get in touch. Please contact Linda Bootherstone at casalinda2006@gmail.com

PREVIOUS PUBLICATIONS
BY
LINDA BOOTHERSTONE

Also available on Amazon

Daisies Don't Tell – An Illustrated Anthology
of Poems
Linda Bick – Xlibris – 2010
ISBN: 978-1-4600-2352-8

Where Angels Fear to Tread – Travel
Autobiography
Linda Bootherstone – Xlibris – 2009
ISBN: 978-1-4415-7931-7

Made in the USA
Columbia, SC
13 March 2018